Table of Contents

Faith, Love, and Sexuality

Jon Marans

Years ago, I dated a Jewish Orthodox gay man and suddenly found myself immersed in his devout religious world of prayers and practices and beliefs—"frum" was how he referred to himself, part of a religious community strictly committed to upholding the 613 commandments of Orthodox Judaism. I knew relatively little about this community, having grown up in a Conservative Jewish household where the practices were quite different. At first I was uncomfortable with my boyfriend's religious routines, but the more he explained things to me, the more I developed a newfound understanding and respect and love for the rituals and commandments of Judaism.

He, however, kept an enormous amount of his life a secret from his frum Jewish community—including our relationship. Here I was in 1990s Manhattan, an out and open gay man and yet feeling as if I had been thrown back into the closet. I had no interest in living this sort of dual and conflicted life. Soon, we were no longer "boyfriends," but friends.

Still, I was fascinated by this smart, successful man who had managed to compartmentalize his life so well—at least to the outside world. However, as his gay relationships and friendships continued and as he grew older and wasn't seriously dating women, he knew he was in the middle of the escalation of an emotional Ponzi scheme which would eventually collapse. But until it did, he had no choice but to keep up his dance of deceit. Unless something rocked his world.

And that's when I first began working on *A Strange and Separate People*, wondering what that event might be.

As with so many plays, that event is grounded in love. And how deeply we love. So much so that we are willing to do crazy, wonderful things that we never could have imagined ourselves doing.

As I began to write this play, I became equally obsessed with the other two characters and their personal journeys—also rocked by love. All three characters are forced to reevaluate what makes them feel right and true and serene at their core and end up making monumental choices because of it. As well as reassessing previously held beliefs.

I also realized that I wrote three characters—Phyllis, Jay, and Stuart —who felt "other than." (An obsession in all of my plays.) Three people who never felt quite part of a group, even though they very much wanted to belong. Having an autistic son, Phyllis felt separated from her Orthodox community; Stuart, an openly gay man, felt disconnected from the New York gay community, disagreeing with what he perceived as their core beliefs; Jay lived a compartmentalized, deceitful life, and because of it, he felt disconnected from both worlds.

During the play, each of these individuals seek new paths to help them be more at peace with themselves and their world. As Stuart—a non-religious Jew—grows more religious, he finds great beauty in the rituals and commandments of Orthodoxy. So much so that he decides by the end of the play to explore reparative therapy. Reparative therapy, which is also referred to as "conversion therapy," is an attempt to change the sexual orientation of a person from homosexual or bisexual to heterosexual. Jay, however, a psychologist who supports reparative therapy as the play begins, comes to a new and different conclusion—that of pride and acceptance of his homosexuality.

The rabbis, leaders, teachers, and professionals of the frum community continue to grapple with the acceptance of homosexuality, homosexual relationships, and the methods and purpose of reparative therapy. In July, 2010, 170 Israeli and American Orthodox rabbis and educators signed a "Statement of Principles on the Place of Jews with a Homosexual Orientation in Our Community," which was a call for greater inclusivity in their religious community. Some people considered this document the beginnings of a long process towards acceptance of homosexuality.

Others strongly disagreed.

In response to this public statement, a "Declaration On The Torah Approach To Homosexuality" was published in 2011. The more than 150 original signers were religious leaders and mental health professionals and believed that the first document gave short shrift to the potential benefits of reparative therapy. It was their argument that Orthodox Jews at least consider trying it to see if it works.

During the off-Broadway run of *A Strange and Separate People*, talk-back sessions were held after performances with members of the cast, crew, and audience members. Side by side of the discussion of the inclusion of homosexuals within the Orthodox Jewish community was the hot-button discussion of reparative therapy. Reparative therapy continues to be an extremely controversial topic for religious leaders and gay men of any faith.

This edition of *A Strange and Separate People* includes additional material to encourage a discussion and understanding of the inner conflicts and personal journeys of men who are gay and are part of an Orthodox Jewish community. Preceding the script are the two differing public statements issued by two differing groups of Jewish leaders. And since each individual's struggle with faith, love, and sexuality is a personal journey, two selected articles have been included as Afterwords.

Statement of Principles on the Place of Jews with a Homosexual Orientation in Our Community

We, the undersigned Orthodox rabbis, *rashei yeshiva, ramim,* Jewish educators and communal leaders affirm the following principles with regard to the place of Jews with a homosexual orientation in our community:

1. All human beings are created in the image of God and deserve to be treated with dignity and respect (*kevod haberiyot*). Every Jew is obligated to fulfill the entire range of mitzvot between person and person in relation to persons who are homosexual or have feelings of same sex attraction. Embarrassing, harassing or demeaning someone with a homosexual orientation or same-sex attraction is a violation of Torah prohibitions that embody the deepest values of Judaism.

2. The question of whether sexual orientation is primarily genetic, or rather environmentally generated, is irrelevant to our obligation to treat human beings with same-sex attractions and orientations with dignity and respect.

3. Halakhah sees heterosexual marriage as the ideal model and sole legitimate outlet for human sexual expression. The sensitivity and understanding we properly express for human beings with other sexual orientations does not diminish our commitment to that principle.

4. Halakhic Judaism views all male and female same-sex sexual interactions as prohibited. The question of whether sexual orientation is primarily genetic, or rather environmentally generated, is irrelevant to this prohibition. While halakha categorizes various homosexual acts with different degrees of severity and opprobrium, including *toeivah,* this does not in any way imply that lesser acts are permitted. But it is critical to emphasize that halakha only prohibits homosexual acts; it does not prohibit orientation or feelings of same-sex attraction, and nothing in the Torah devalues the human beings who struggle with them. (We do not here address the issue of *hirhurei aveirah,* a halakhic category that goes beyond mere feelings and applies to all forms of sexuality and requires precise halakhic definition.)

5. Whatever the origin or cause of homosexual orientation, many individuals believe that for most people this orientation cannot be changed. Others believe that for most people it is a matter of free will. Similarly, while

some mental health professionals and rabbis in the community strongly believe in the efficacy of "change therapies", most of the mental health community, many rabbis, and most people with a homosexual orientation feel that some of these therapies are either ineffective or potentially damaging psychologically for many patients.

We affirm the religious right of those with a homosexual orientation to reject therapeutic approaches they reasonably see as useless or dangerous.

6. Jews with a homosexual orientation who live in the Orthodox community confront serious emotional, communal and psychological challenges that cause them and their families great pain and suffering. For example, homosexual orientation may greatly increase the risk of suicide among teenagers in our community. Rabbis and communities need to be sensitive and empathetic to that reality. Rabbis and mental health professionals must provide responsible and ethical assistance to congregants and clients dealing with those human challenges.

7. Jews struggling to live their lives in accordance with halakhic values need and deserve our support. Accordingly, we believe that the decision as to whether to be open about one's sexual orientation should be left to such individuals, who should consider their own needs and those of the community. We are opposed on ethical and moral grounds to both the "outing" of individuals who want to remain private and to coercing those who desire to be open about their orientation to keep it hidden.

8. Accordingly, Jews with homosexual orientations or same sex-attractions should be welcomed as full members of the synagogue and school community. As appropriate with regard to gender and lineage, they should participate and count ritually, be eligible for ritual synagogue honors, and generally be treated in the same fashion and under the same halakhic and hashkafic framework as any other member of the synagogue they join. Conversely, they must accept and fulfill all the responsibilities of such membership, including those generated by communal norms or broad Jewish principles that go beyond formal halakha.

We do not here address what synagogues should do about accepting members who are openly practicing homosexuals and/or living with a same-sex partner. Each synagogue together with its rabbi must establish its own standard with regard to membership for open violators of halakha. Those standards should be applied fairly and objectively.

9. Halakha articulates very exacting criteria and standards of eligibility for particular religious offices, such as officially appointed cantor during the year or *baal tefillah* on the High Holidays. Among the most important of those criteria is that the entire congregation must be fully comfortable with having that person serve as its representative. This legitimately prevents even the most admirable individuals, who are otherwise perfectly fit halakhically, from serving in those roles. It is the responsibility of the lay and rabbinic leadership in each individual community to determine eligibility for those offices in line with those principles, the importance of maintaining communal harmony, and the unique context of its community culture.

10. Jews with a homosexual orientation or same sex attraction, even if they engage in same sex interactions, should be encouraged to fulfill *mitzvot* to the best of their ability. All Jews are challenged to fulfill *mitzvot* to the best of their ability, and the attitude of "all or nothing" was not the traditional approach adopted by the majority of halakhic thinkers and *poskim* throughout the ages.

11. Halakhic Judaism cannot give its blessing and imprimatur to Jewish religious same-sex commitment ceremonies and weddings, and halakhic values proscribe individuals and communities from encouraging practices that grant religious legitimacy to gay marriage and couplehood. But communities should display sensitivity, acceptance and full embrace of the adopted or biological children of homosexually active Jews in the synagogue and school setting, and we encourage parents and family of homosexually partnered Jews to make every effort to maintain harmonious family relations and connections.

12. Jews who have an exclusively homosexual orientation should, under most circumstances, not be encouraged to marry someone of the other gender, as this can lead to great tragedy, unrequited love, shame, dishonesty and ruined lives. They should be directed to contribute to Jewish and general society in other meaningful ways. Any such person who is planning to marry someone of the opposite gender is halakhically and ethically required to fully inform his or her potential spouse of their sexual orientation.

We hope and pray that by sharing these thoughts we will help the Orthodox community to fully live out its commitment to the principles and values of Torah and Halakha as practiced and cherished by the children of Abraham, who our sages teach us are recognized by the qualities of being *rahamanim* (merciful), *bayshanim* (modest), and *gomelei hasadim* engaging in acts of loving-kindness).

Declaration On The Torah Approach To Homosexuality

On December 26, 2011 a coalition of more than 150 Orthodox rabbis, community organizers and leaders, and mental-health professionals released a public statement declaring that the only Torah-approved course of action with regard to homosexuality was psychological therapy coupled with teshuva, or repentance.

The document, entitled "Declaration on the Torah Approach to Homosexuality," sought to clarify the theological understanding of the Biblically mandated prohibition. It also presented what the authors and signers saw as a practical and achievable solution for those faced with same-sex attractions. Its position was that same-sex attractions could be modified and healed.

The Declaration was written by a twenty-five-member committee consisting of rabbis, parents, "strugglers" (those still undergoing therapy), and "success stories" (those who underwent therapy and are living heterosexual lives, many with spouses and children). According to a press release issued by www.TorahDec.org, members of the committee authoring the statement requested anonymity. Below is a full copy of the public statement.

Declaration On The Torah Approach To Homosexuality

Societal Developments On Homosexuality

There has been a monumental shift in the secular world's attitude towards homosexuality over the past few decades. In particular over the past fifteen years there has been a major public campaign to gain acceptance for homosexuality. Legalizing same-sex marriage has become the end goal of the campaign to equate homosexuality with heterosexuality.

A propaganda blitz has been sweeping the world using political tactics to persuade the public about the legitimacy of homosexuality. The media is rife with negative labels implying that one is "hateful" or "homophobic" if they do not accept the homosexual lifestyle as legitimate. This political coercion has silenced many into acquiescence. Unfortunately this attitude has seeped into the Torah community and many have become confused or have accepted the media's portrayal of this issue.

The Torah's Unequivocal And Eternal Message

The Torah makes a clear statement that homosexuality is not an acceptable lifestyle or a genuine identity by severely prohibiting its conduct. Furthermore, the Torah, ever prescient about negative secular influences, warns us in Vayikra (Leviticus) 20:23 "Do not follow the traditions of the nations that I expel from before you..." Particularly the Torah writes this in regards to homosexuality and other forbidden sexual liaisons.

Same-Sex Attractions Can Be Modified And Healed

From a Torah perspective, the question whether homosexual inclinations and behaviors are changeable is extremely relevant. The concept that G-d created a human being who is unable to find happiness in a loving relationship unless he violates a biblical prohibition is neither plausible nor acceptable. G-d is loving and merciful. Struggles, and yes, difficult struggles, along with healing and personal growth are part and parcel of this world. Impossible, life long, Torah prohibited situations with no achievable solutions are not.

We emphatically reject the notion that a homosexually inclined person cannot overcome his or her inclination and desire. Behaviors are changeable. The Torah does not forbid something which is impossible to avoid. Abandoning people to lifelong loneliness and despair by denying all hope of overcoming and healing their same-sex attraction is heartlessly cruel. Such an attitude also violates the biblical prohibition in Vayikra (Leviticus) 19:14 "and you shall not place a stumbling block before the blind."

The Process Of Healing

The only viable course of action that is consistent with the Torah is therapy and teshuvah. The therapy consists of reinforcing the natural gender-identity of the individual by helping him or her understand and repair the emotional wounds that led to its disorientation and weakening, thus enabling the resumption and completion of the individual's emotional development. Teshuvah is a Torah-mandated, self-motivated process of turning away from any transgression or sin and returning to G-d and one's spiritual essence. This includes refining and reintegrating the personality and allowing it to grow in a healthy and wholesome manner.

These processes are typically facilitated and coordinated with the help of a specially trained counselor or therapist working in conjunction with a qualified spiritual teacher or guide. There is no other practical, Torah-sanctioned solution for this issue.

The Mitzvah Of Love And Compassion

It requires tremendous bravery and fortitude for a person to confront and deal with same-sex attraction. For example a sixteen-year-old who is struggling with this issue may be confused and afraid and not know whom to speak to or what steps to take. We must create an atmosphere where this teenager (or anyone) can speak freely to a parent, rabbi, or mentor and be treated with love and compassion. Authority figures can then guide same-sex struggl towards a path of healing and overcoming their inclinations.

The key point to remember is that these individuals are primarily innocent victims of childhood emotional wounds. They deserve our full love, support and encouragement in their striving towards healing. Struggling individuals who seek health and wellness should not be confused with the homosexual movement and their agenda. This distinction is crucial. It reflects the difference between what G-d asks from all of us and what He unambiguously prohibits.

We need to do everything in our power to lovingly uplift struggling individuals towards a full and healthy life that is filled with love, joy and the wisdom of the Torah.

A STRANGE AND SEPARATE PEOPLE
PRODUCTION HISTORY

A Strange and Separate People was originally produced by the Penguin Repertory Company in Stony Point, New York on October 6, 2005.   Executive director, Andrew M. Horn and the artistic director, Joe Brancato. It was directed by Joe Brancato; set design by Jason Courson; costume designs by A. Christina Giannini; lighting design by Jeff Croiter; sound design by Johnna Doty. The production stage manager was Jack McDowell; properties, Sheila Ann Fass. The cast was as follows:

JAY BERMAN...Sam Guncler
PHYLLIS BERMAN .... Patricia Randell
STUART WEINSTEIN...................................Arnie Burton

A scene from the Penguin Repertory Company production of *A Strange and Separate People* with Patricia Randell and Sam Guncler.
Photo by Kerwin McCarthy

16

Scenes from the Penguin Repertory Company production of *A Strange and Separate People* with Sam Guncler and Arnie Burton. Photo by Kerwin McCarthy

Scenes from the off-Broadway production of *A Strange and Separate People*. Top left: Noah Weisberg and Tricia Paolucci; Top right: Jonathan Hammond; Center left: Jonathan Hammond and Tricia Paoluccio; Bottom: Noah Weisberg and Jonathan Hammond. Photos by Michael Portantiere/FollowSpotPhoto.com

A scene from the off-Broadway production of *A Strange and Separate People*.
From left to right: Noah Weisberg, Tricia Paoluccio, and Jonathan Hammond.
Photo by Michael Portantiere/FollowSpotPhoto.com

A Strange and Separate People was produced in New York City by Stacy Shane at the Studio Theatre on Theatre Row, performances beginning on July 14, 2011. The executive producer was Daryl Roth. The general management was Adam Hess, DR Theatrical Management; the company manager was Kyle Provost. It was directed by Jeff Calhoun; set and costume designs were by Clint Ramos; lighting design by Ryan O'Gara; sound design by Jill B.C. DuBoff; graphic design by Adrian Sie; casting by Stephanie Klapper. The production stage manager was Julie DeRossi; assistant stage manager was Aaron Elgart. The press rep was Kevin P. McAnarney. The cast was as follows:

JAY BERMAN..Jonathan Hammond
PHYLLIS BERMAN .... Tricia Paoluccio
STUART WEINSTEIN....................................Noah Weisberg

One of the revolutionary things about Judaism is that
it teaches us to be thankful for the every day blessings
in our lives not just the new or unexpected ones.

This play is dedicated to eight people who I am routinely grateful for:
Alvin Deutsch
Gail Marans
David Marans
Jim Sapp
Adam Hess
Kyle Provost
Alexander Fraser
and
Daryl Roth

A Strange and Separate People

CHARACTERS

STUART WEINSTEIN, early 30s, is a ridiculously handsome, cocky, driven, Jewish (but-coolly controlled, WASPy-acting) doctor. Has a sly, dry wit and is a bit of a bad boy.

PHYLLIS BERMAN, early-mid 30s, attractive. While she has a slightly private, almost proper demeanor, underneath she's a pit-bull. Though somewhat prudish, she has a deep reservoir of enjoying the absurdities of life.

JAY BERMAN, Phyllis' husband, 30s, is a tough, good looking, high energy, wildly charismatic, self-centered man.

TIME

The Present

PLACE

A simple, non-realistic set where the floor/carpet appears to be a wild, multi-colored splash painting which crawls half-way up the walls. There's a table with a few chairs around it. Maybe a couple of large children's blocks on either side of the space. Other than that, there should be as little as possible on the stage.

AUTHOR'S NOTE

After each scene of the play, there are non-verbal sections which are vital to help move the story and the character development along. Please consider these non-verbal sections as important as the dialogue. Further, with the aid of a non-realistic set and the elimination of most blackouts, these non-verbal sections should hopefully flow directly out of these scenes without the action ever stopping.

On a different note: While this play involves religious people, none of them are saints. All of them cross lines and do inappropriate things--sometimes even relish their improprieties. These are three people stumbling through life trying to do the right thing, yet often not. I encourage actors to embrace the many sides of these smart, fun, manipulative, exasperating, endearing people.

More than anything, Jay, Stuart, and Phyllis are three extremely curious people who have an enormous love of learning.
Stuart and Phyllis were both born in Manhattan and have basic "American" accents. Jay, having grown up in a lower middle class New York home, might have a slight 'tough guy' Brooklyn accent.

Finally, please note that whenever G-d's name is referenced in the play during prayers, the script has utilized the terms "Hashem" or "Elokeinu" or "Hallelukah". This choice has been made in adherence to the Third Commandment which states: "You shall not take the name of the Lord your G-d in vain." Judaism interprets this commandment as precluding speaking the name of G-d except during actual prayer or when making a blessing. It remains the author's preference that, out of a show of respect for those beliefs, all productions use only the pseudonyms referenced above in place of G-d's name.

"We (the Queen Mother and I) talked about Jews for a bit and she said she liked them very much but they were a separate people and a strange people, keeping to themselves and their own ways."

Printed in the *Diaries of Woodrow Wyatt*, a friend of the Queen Mother

A Strange and Separate People

A light splashes up on Jay, talking to audience.

JAY. Feel your feet against the ground. Touching the earth ... Good. Now press your feet together. (*Demonstrating. Someone in the audience is complaining.*) *However* you want! Just do it. Stop whining! Whatever's comfortable. Heel against heel. Sole against sole.

(*Another part of the stage, another splash of light. Phyllis talks to a child as if he's out in the audience. Phyllis' hands are behind her back.*)

PHYLLIS. (*Loudly talking to child, serious.*) No laughing right now. Where's the shoe? (*Child guesses wrong. Shows fork from behind her hands, frustrated.*) That's the fork.

JAY. (*To audience.*) Enjoy the sensation that "hey, look at that—my feet are touching each other."

(*Another area—a brushstroke of light splashes onto Stuart.*)

STUART. (*In his own thoughts, concerned.*) Touching. Yes.

JAY. (*In his own world, to audience.*) It's a nice feeling. I mean after all—your left foot likes your right foot. (*Acting concerned.*) Right?

STUART. (*His own thoughts.*) But separate. Touching, but—

PHYLLIS. (*To a child in audience, hiding them behind her.*) Here's the shoe in my right hand—the fork in my left. Now I'm holding them behind me. WHERE'S THE SHOE?!

STUART. (*Knowing what he must do.*) But separate.

JAY. So what if you don't get that feeling today. A little secret—it ain't so easy to make two into one. Just—let 'em keep touching. Something will happen.

(*Lights fade down on all of them and crossfade up on ...*

Jay and Phyllis' Upper West side living room. The most prominent item is a rug which was originally one solid color, but has been scrawled and splashed on with multi-colored crayons and magic markers. The walls are also crayoned and painted on with splashes of color but only to about three feet high up. It's early afternoon. We hear the sound of a child laughing.)

PHYLLIS. *(Offstage, loudly talking to someone, serious.)* Now where's the shoe?! *(Stunned, thrilled.)* Good. In the right hand! Good! Let's try it again. In my left hand … And in my right—*(Sound of intercom buzzer. Phyllis instructs someone in the other room.)* Keep doing 'shoe and fork' with him. *(Still offstage, Phyllis answers intercom phone.)* Yes? … But it's no where near two o'clock. (Listens on phone) 1:57? Well … uh—send him up— *(Exasperated.)* You already did?

(Phyllis hangs up the phone just as her doorbell buzzes. She enters the room, wearing a nice, simple dress—although something is off about it. It hasn't been pressed or ironed. And her hair is somewhat disheveled.)

PHYLLIS. Coming.

(Phyllis opens the door for Stuart Weinstein, immaculately dressed. She stares at him, taken aback at how handsome he is. He stares at her equally intensely. FYI—In this scene they must never touch. Orthodox Jews of the opposite sex never touch, not even shaking hands with each other.)

STUART. *(Somewhat uneasy.)* … Hello. I'm—Stuart Weinstein.

PHYLLIS. Phyllis Berman. And I am *so* sorry. *(Stuart looks puzzled.)* About the hideous state of my hair … *(Looks at her dress.)* And my dress.

STUART. *(Noticing.)* I didn't notice.

PHYLLIS. You—are a terrible liar … Yes. *(She looks at him for a moment.)* I feel especially ratty in comparison to what you're wearing. Quite a beautiful suit.

STUART. I suppose.

PHYLLIS. No. I think you know it. *(Stuart laughs.)* Do you realize you're very punctual?

STUART. *(Proud of it)* I should hope so. *(Beat)* I'm here about having a party catered.

PHYLLIS. *(Puzzled he'd say that.)* I know. *I* booked the appointment. Can I get you something to drink?

STUART. *(With an odd conviction.)* I don't drink anymore.

PHYLLIS. *(Again she's surprised)* Uh…I meant orange juice. Water.

STUART. I'm fine.

(In the next room we hear the gleeful sound of a young boy.)

PHYLLIS. Not to worry. My son.

STUART. *(Surprised.)* You have a son?

PHYLLIS. *(Again puzzled)* Well—yes. *(Another gleeful cry from her son.)* Gail is in there—looking after him. She is a blessing.

STUART. He sounds rambunctious.

PHYLLIS. *(Suspicious)* And you have a problem with that?

STUART. No.

PHYLLIS. I've carpeted all the rooms and sound-proofed his walls. Are you a friend of the Ukrainian woman below me?

STUART. This is my first time in the building.

(Beat.)

PHYLLIS. *(Calming down.)* Sorry. Take a seat. Tell me what kind of party you want catered. I'm amazed you found me. I haven't exactly done a lot of catering these days.

(*Stuart looks at a chair stained with added splashes of color.*)

STUART. I'll stand.

PHYLLIS. Ethan—my son.

STUART. (*Looking at chair, carpet.*) Vibrant colors.

PHYLLIS. (*Pointing out colors.*) Mostly from his crayons. Though here's some grape juice. Pizza? Actually I may have done that!

STUART. He clearly has a lot of energy. (*Looking up.*) Even the walls.

PHYLLIS. Which is why I don't hang any paintings. I hate the walls being bare, but— There was this style of painting I *really* loved—called Fauvism—

STUART. Yes, I know it—

PHYLLIS. (*Overlapping*) —it flourished in the South of France. All paint was applied directly from the paint tubes *right* onto the canvas—

STUART. —because the goal was to use only pure, raw colors.

PHYLLIS. (*Surprised.*) … That's right.

STUART. Matisse was in that group.

PHYLLIS. (*Again surprised.*) The father of the movement! And because the paint was applied straight from the paint tubes—the canvases—at least for me—had a dynamic, sensual … feel to them. (*It's a little uncomfortable and inappropriate that she is making this conversation a tad sexual. And yet for some reason she continues on.*) … Don't you think?

(*Beat. As Stuart thinks that over, he is aware of the unease and sexual tension in the air. Although Stuart, being so handsome, is used to it.*)

STUART. Yes … Sensual … Almost—animalistic.

PHYLLIS. … Yes.

STUART. Like they're almost clawing their way off the canvas.

PHYLLIS. *(Nervous laughter.)* … And because these paintings were so passionate, the painters were called "Les Fauves." The Wild—

STUART. The Wild beasts. *(Stuart pretends to be painting with passion, growling as he does it.)* Grrr … Grrr …

PHYLLIS. *(He's being inappropriate.)* You should—uh—stop.

(He does.)

STUART. … A few years ago, I binged on art—hanging out at galleries all over the city.

PHYLLIS. Weren't you the lucky one? I haven't gone in years.

STUART. *(Oddly personal.)* I like to really immerse myself into something. But then suddenly, that's it. Had enough.

PHYLLIS. Oh, like your drinking. *(Stuart's taken aback.)* So this binging, would you say it's a good or bad thing?

STUART. *(Stunned at her bluntness.)* Hmm. Well, it *does* help me move on to newer passions and projects.

PHYLLIS. Interesting how you turn a negative into a positive … Good for you

STUART. I'm impressed … how much you know about Fauvism.

PHYLLIS. I was an art historian … until Ethan … *(Looking at the walls.)* It would have been nice to have a few Fauvist prints …

(Stuart looks at the rug and walls.)

STUART. In a way, you already do. From your son. And they certainly have a lot of passion in them. *(Hearing Ethan's noises in other room.)* Actually, *he* sounds passionate as well.

PHYLLIS. Especially when he's hungry! Never turn your back on him at the dinner table or your meal will be gone!

STUART. That clinches it. You have your very own little Fauve! Your own little Beast!

PHYLLIS. … My son is just as human as any other child.

STUART. I didn't say he wasn't.

PHYLLIS. Just because he's autistic doesn't mean he can't be a great artist.

STUART. *(Stunned)* … I had no idea your son—He could certainly *still* be a great artist.

PHYLLIS. Don't patronize me.

STUART. I wouldn't. *(Trying to sound sincere, but coming off a bit pompous.)* Did I tell you that I am a doctor?

PHYLLIS. In my experience, most doctors think G-d works for *them*. *(Suddenly there's a pounding sound from below.)* Excuse me. *(Phyllis goes to a spot on the floor that isn't carpeted, stomps her foot once, then explains to Stuart.)* The Ukrainian woman … Sorry—for being rude. It was wrong of me. Still I do it. What is that about? … Let's get back to your party. How many guests are you expecting?

STUART. You don't need to apologize. You have a lot going on in your life.

PHYLLIS. Cooped up all the time. And just the other day, this woman— *(Realizing she's going on, embarrassed.)* So how many guests?

STUART. … Two dozen.

PHYLLIS. I thought you said fifty on the phone.

STUART. Did I? ... I've been going back and forth. *(From the other room, they hear Ethan again. This time it's hard to tell if it's a laugh or a cry. The sound appears almost less than human. Phyllis feels a little uncomfortable that Stuart heard this.)* What happened? With the women? ... I want to hear. *(Off Phyllis' look.)* No patronizing.

(Beat. Something about this man makes her continue on.)

PHYLLIS. I was on the M104 bus, heading uptown, trying to calm Ethan. But couldn't. This woman leans over—starts yelling at me—saying what a terrible mother I am. That I'm lazy—can't control my child.

STUART. *(Indignant.)* And you said?

PHYLLIS. Nothing. At first. But she wouldn't stop berating me until I finally said, "my son is autistic and I can't stop the screaming—as much as I would love to!" And then the woman starts bawling. Like a little cry baby. Apologizing over and over.

STUART. *That* seems nice.

PHYLLIS. Except I had to go through being yelled at to begin with!

STUART. Unfortunately, a lot of people are pigs.

PHYLLIS. I don't know about that.

STUART. Selfish, inconsiderate pigs.

PHYLLIS. *(Thinking this through.)* ... Yes, they are.

STUART. Except ... *(Off Phyllis' puzzlement, flirtatious.)* ... us.

(They both laugh. She's definitely captivated by this man.)

PHYLLIS. That really IS a beautiful suit. Looks like you stepped out of the Bloomies catalogue. You almost look like one of the models. Handsome. Aloof. Emotionally distant.

31

STUART. Uh ... thanks?

PHYLLIS. I never think of them being Jewish. But here you are. I'll bet your girlfriends have been very beautiful ... Or your wives.

STUART. *(Amused.)* You assume I've been married—and more than once?

PHYLLIS. You just look like you might have been.

STUART. I've never been married. Although I've had a lot of boyfriends. Some fairly handsome. A few even chiseled.

PHYLLIS. *(Stunned.)* ... Is that a joke?

STUART. *(Sadly.)* Just the chiseled part.

PHYLLIS. *(Puzzled and a little uncomfortable as to why Stuart is here.)* You do know I'm an *orthodox* caterer.

STUART. Well, since the name of your company *is* "Phyllis's Orthodox Catering"—Not the catchiest of names.

PHYLLIS. *You're* orthodox as well?

STUART. *(Proudly)* That's right. A baltshuvah. (*Trans: someone newly religious.*)

PHYLLIS. *(Looking down on baltshuvahs.)* Oh a baltshuvah. How recently did you become frum— *(Translating.)* religious?

STUART. I know frum means religious ... I started—uh— "reacquainting" myself with Judaism about six months ago.

PHYLLIS. So your family was originally religious?

STUART. My grandfather. My Dad was basically a High Holiday Jew. Went to synagogue twice on a year—on the—uh—high holidays.

PHYLLIS. That's not a Jew.

STUART. ... Okay.

PHYLLIS. Well, at least to me....And *you're* Orthodox and gay?

STUART. Yes.

PHYLLIS. This is a first for me. *(Not pleased, but trying to hide it.)* And to be so open about it.

STUART. I'm planning on being the first of a new breed of gay orthodox men. Discreet, but open.

PHYLLIS. You do realize that homosexuality goes against the laws of the Torah.

STUART. *(Said quite seriously, professionally, as only a doctor would say it.)* Only anal intercourse ... The Torah says a man shall not lie with a man the way he does with a woman. In the commentaries, Rashi says that means anal penetration. So if I don't do any of that, I'm okay. Blessed by Rashi no less! *(Eagerly, like a little boy.)* I'll show you the passage. I always carry it with me!

PHYLLIS. I believe you ... And that's the way *you're* interpreting Rashi.

STUART. I'm hardly the only one. *(Off her look.)* I am hardly the only one.

PHYLLIS. *(Enjoying the argument.)* ... You call yourself frum, but you're not wearing a yarmulke.

STUART. That's a very public statement for me to suddenly make in front of my patients.

PHYLLIS. Oh, so when it comes to being religious, you're still in the closet!

STUART. ... Touché.

PHYLLIS. *(Tickled.)* I thought it was clever myself. *(They laugh. Then Stuart looks over the place.)*

STUART. *(Realizing.)* You could still put up some Fauvist prints. Just hang them extra high.

PHYLLIS. Ethan's getting taller. Besides, that would look a little strange.

STUART. *(Said innocently.)* Why should you care? Not as if you're closeted when it comes to letting people know about your son. *(Phyllis is silent.)* Are you?

(She is, but doesn't want to admit it.)

PHYLLIS. There's already enough beauty in my apartment. From Ethan. His brown wavy hair. Big brown eyes. All the doctors say that for some reason, autistic children tend to be quite good-looking. Something G-d did to compensate, I suppose. *(Realizing.)* Huh.

STUART. What?

PHYLLIS. *(Excited about her theory.)* Maybe G-d did the same thing for you. Made you so handsome to compensate for your being gay! Certainly a high percentage of gay men are also quite nice looking.

STUART. Because they keep themselves in good shape.

PHYLLIS. That could help. But still, I think there's something to it.

STUART. *(Disagrees.)* Perhaps.

PHYLLIS. You have to admit, right or wrong, it *is* an interesting theory.

STUART. And a tad bigoted.

PHYLLIS. Oh no argument there. Show me a person who isn't a tad bigoted and judgmental—and I'll show you someone who has no opinions. Or backbone.

(Beat.)

STUART. *(Hating to admit it, but…)* Sometimes even *I* find the gay world — *(changing subject)* Your son — how extreme is his autism? Does he talk?

PHYLLIS. Not really. And he's seven. Almost eight. Still, I work with him every day. He's learning.

STUART. And retains it?

PHYLLIS. Not as much as some other autistic children. Because he refuses to concentrate! Still, I work with him. He has a wonderful spirit. Although … these last few weeks …

(She stops, thinking she's said too much.)

STUART. His behavior has changed?

PHYLLIS. *(Surprised he knew.)* He's started hitting me. And Gail. Scratched a few of the kids at his school.

STUART. Have you taken him to a doctor?

PHYLLIS. Countless.

STUART. Did any of them check for a yeast infection?

PHYLLIS. No.

STUART. Have you gone to a gastro-enterologist?

PHYLLIS. That's what you are?

STUART. *(He is.)* Some autistic children — especially if they're always putting things into their mouths —

PHYLLIS. Yes, that's Ethan! Twigs and leaves on the ground, crayons —

STUART. Chances are good he's developed some nasty digestive problem. They're extremely painful.

PHYLLIS. Painful? Oh I see. And of course he wouldn't be able to tell me that.

STUART. But the good news—usually medication clears it right up. So—uh—if you want to bring him to my office—

PHYLLIS. Of course I do! … If this is taken care of, will it help him improve in other ways?

STUART. Other ways?

PHYLLIS. With his mind.

STUART. (*Stating the facts.*) No.

PHYLLIS. (*From strength, determined.*) … Still, I work with him every day. Trying all the different techniques. That's helping. (*Realizing.*) In a way, I'm making my own Fauvist painting—splashing a million ideas out at Ethan—hoping all the colors will come together.

STUART. … How's your—uh—husband managing?

PHYLLIS. (*With an attitude.*) Jay—that's his name. He thinks I'm doing too much. That I should accept our son the way he is. Have blind faith. *Maybe* there's something to it. One day Jay walks into the apartment—absentmindedly drops his coat on the floor, then walks off. A few hours later, he comes back into the living room. Ethan's drawn all over his coat—a design like the one on this carpet. Then hands it to my husband. *Actually* hands it to him. (*Touch of bitterness.*) Ethan's never handed a gift to me … I tell Jay—dry clean it out. He says he likes it the way it is. It reminds him of Joseph's coat of many colors.

STUART. That's kind of sweet … although inaccurate. Joseph's coat of many colors was a gift of honor that a father gave to his son. In this case, it's a son giving it to his father.

PHYLLIS. (Not pleased.) … Each time we step outside, Jay proudly wears that coat. (Confiding.) Sometimes I end up walking a couple of steps behind him. People notice … that coat. Jay doesn't care. Jay doesn't even mind the carpet being—He likes it … I mean I'm proud of my child as much as Jay—

STUART. Sometimes you're not 100% proud because you know it can be better. I feel that way about Orthodoxy.

PHYLLIS. Yes, that makes perfect sense! … For you. (Pointed.) Of course at what point do you learn to accept what can't be better—and embrace it anyway?

STUART. (Referring to her son.) That's trickier. For all of us.

PHYLLIS. (Changing subject.) … But you came here to talk about catering an affair. Not my life. What kind of affair did you say you were having?

STUART. I think it's changing every day.

PHYLLIS. Not unusual.

STUART. (Taking out wallet.) Here's my card. If you'd like to come by for a consultation.

PHYLLIS. (She looks at the card of this M.D.) A shame you don't have a woman in your life—to make you happy.

STUART. But not a man?

(Another cry is heard offstage. And the sound of a thud.)

PHYLLIS. I'd better check on that.

(As Phyllis grabs a box of cookies and exits offstage, the pounding from the Ukrainian woman begins again. Stuart starts to call out to Phyllis, but instead—in solidarity—he stomps his foot down—pounding back at the Ukrainian woman.

Lights swiftly fade down on the room and then strictly come back up on Stuart. He takes a yarmulke out of his pocket and places it on his head. Then he seductively takes off his jacket and rolls up his sleeves. This moment should have an oddly disturbing and disquieting feel to it. As lights come up on the entire room, we now find ourselves back in ...

Jay and Phyllis' Apartment. A few weeks later. It's Friday evening.{If the Sabbath candles are in the room, they'd already be lit—so it's probably best not to include them in this scene.} Phyllis enters carrying in three small cups of soup for the Sabbath meal. She is dressed considerably better than before. As she enters, Stuart exits and reenters bringing in the Kiddish cup, the wine, the prayer books.

Stuart and Phyllis have become friendlier these last few weeks and it shows.)

STUART. *(Speaks during the above as they enter and reenter.)* Well I simply don't believe you. You *must* have one favorite part.

PHYLLIS. Really. For me, the *entire* Shabbos meal is beautiful.

STUART. Not just beautiful. Something that ... I don't know ... makes you smile every time you get to it.

PHYLLIS. Makes me smile? Oh, the prayer for the wine.

STUART. Going right for the liquor.

(Phyllis reenters, bringing in the bread which sits on the challah board.)

PHYLLIS. No. Not at all. Oh you! ... One of the *first* prayers is the blessing for the wine. Only a couple of minutes later do we finally say the prayer for the bread.

STUART. Correct.

PHYLLIS. *(Demonstrating with bread.)* Well I just love the fact that we cover the bread with a napkin or cloth—so the bread won't overhear that the prayer for the wine is being said first!

STUART. Because?

PHYLLIS. We don't want the bread to feel hurt—that it's not first in the pecking order of blessings.

STUART. *(Amused.)* Oh.

PHYLLIS. *(Not amused.)* It teaches children that other people's feelings are important.

STUART. Even if the other person is only a loaf of bread.

PHYLLIS. Excuse me, but it shows if we care that much about bread, how much more should we care about people.

STUART. … That *is* nice.

PHYLLIS. Although most of us haven't really learned from the bread. Even orthodox children. The way they sometimes treat …

(Phyllis gets quiet, upset at the way they treat Ethan. Stuart sees this.)

STUART. *(In a wry, comforting way.)* Unfortunately, a lot of people are—

STUART/PHYLLIS. Pigs.

STUART. What can I bring out next?

PHYLLIS. I'm fine.

STUART. All of our lunches here, you barely let me help.

PHYLLIS. Too bad. Can't always have everything your way. *(Phyllis looks at Stuart affectionately, then breaks away knowing she is crossing a line.)* Did I tell you that when I hid the fork and the shoe this afternoon, Ethan picked the right one eight out of ten times?

STUART. *(She did and more than once.)* Yes, you did … And that was a great example before. About what makes you smile on Shabbos. The bread … I wonder if anyone else in this room has a great example.

PHYLLIS. (*Amused.*) Oh—and you? What makes you smile on Shabbos—

STUART. The song *"Eyshet chayil"* —"The Woman of Valor." One of the few times Judaism *demands* that the husband thank his wife for all the hard work she's done.

PHYLLIS. That is so sweet of you to pick that song.

STUART. …It certainly is. (*Stuart moves in to touch Phyllis' cheek. She moves back. In orthodoxy, men and women who aren't married or related shouldn't touch each other.*) From the cooking—You must have had— (*And although it isn't allowed, he wipes something off of Phyllis' cheek. The moment is electric for her.*) Gone … Sure there's nothing else I can do to help?

PHYLLIS. Sit down. I just need to check on the food. (He starts to follow her anyway) … No! Stay there. (*Phyllis goes offstage as they continue speaking.*) I have a feeling Jay will enjoy meeting you. He loves colorful people.

STUART. Where's Ethan tonight?

PHYLLIS. (*Offstage.*) With my parents for the weekend. And he went without a struggle. No kicking. Or screaming … I know I've thanked you a million times, but that medication you prescribed for him—it's almost sane here again. It still amazes me—you came here to have something catered—(*Suddenly remembering, as she enters.*) I keep forgetting to ask. What happened to that party you wanted?

STUART. It was pushed back.

(*Jay enters from a long day, wearing the Coat of Many Colors and carrying in a shopping bag. Before Jay even sees Stuart, Stuart begins to speak.*)

STUART. Oh, why hello there! I'm Stuart Weinstein. You must be Jay. I'm a friend of your wife's. She invited me over for Shabbos.

JAY. ... Welcome. It's a mitzvah to share the Shabbos with strangers.

PHYLLIS. I thought I'd surprise you.

JAY. Well done.

STUART. That is a wild and beautiful coat. I hear your son made it for you.

JAY. (*Surprised this stranger knows this.*) ... That's correct.

(*Jay starts to drop his coat on the floor.*)

PHYLLIS. (*Grabs his coat, hangs it on a hook on the wall.*) Let me help you with that, Jay ... Stuart is the doctor I told you about—who helped clear up Ethan's infection.

JAY. Oh. I'm glad I can finally thank you in person. (*Beat.*) Thank you. (*To Phyllis.*) I didn't realize the two of you had become so friendly outside of his office.

PHYLLIS. Oh, yes. He's dragged me to tons of museums.

STUART. The Guggenheim is our favorite.

PHYLLIS. Whichever we go to, I seem to like.

STUART. I feel the same. Because of the company. (*To Jay.*) Phyllis knows so many things about art. *And* religion. Because of her, I now wear my yarmulke out in public.

PHYLLIS. (*A little embarrassed she has done so much with Stuart.*) Guilty as charged.

JAY. (*To Phyllis.*) You never told me about any of this.

PHYLLIS/STUART. No?

JAY. (*To Phyllis.*) No.

PHYLLIS. *(Privately tickled.)* Are you jealous?

JAY. Do I have reason to be?

PHYLLIS. Stuart is orthodox.

JAY. Orthodox men don't fool around?

STUART. We'd like to think not.

PHYLLIS. Stuart is also—gay. So he wouldn't be fooling around with me … And a baltshuvah.

JAY. Oh. And a born again Jew. *(Off Stuart's glance.)* Just making a joke.

PHYLLIS. Jay actually has had a couple of clients in your situation. Religious and gay. I told you he's a psychologist, right?

STUART. Yes. *(To Jay.)* So you help those clients embrace their sexuality?

(Jay and Phyllis try not to laugh.)

JAY. Very funny.

STUART. If you don't help them embrace their sexuality, exactly what do you do to them?

JAY. Do *to* them? … I don't think you really want to hear about it.

STUART. Actually, you're wrong—

PHYLLIS. Go on, Jay. He wants to know.

(Beat.)

JAY. These particular clients who come to me are religious men.

STUART. Like me.

(Phyllis and Jay try not to chuckle again.)

JAY. No. *These* men are desperately trying to get rid of their unwanted same sex attraction.

STUART. You make it sound like dandruff ... Or lice.

PHYLLIS. *(Seriously.)* Actually, that's what it *is*—to them.

JAY. They're not interested in being part of your homosexual community. Because they're not gay. Their problem—they've got Same Sex Attraction Disorder.

STUART. And you think you can cure this ... disorder?

PHYLLIS. If they're willing to work at it.

STUART. No matter what, they'll always be physically turned on by men.

PHYLLIS. Actually that's not—

JAY. *(Interrupting Phyllis.)* Not true at all. Because some were never sexually "turned on" by men to begin with.

STUART. Oh really?

JAY. These poor guys—a lot of them had lousy masculine role models growing up. Some of them were bullied or ridiculed by other boys—or even by their dads—because they were different. Maybe they were lousy in sports. Or had a more sensitive nature. Whatever. It made them feel like that they weren't real men. And it didn't help that other boys wouldn't hang out with them. All of this rejection made them feel disconnected from other guys. And from their dad. Then—around puberty —this incredible *need* for hetero male bonding and companionship became sexualized.

PHYLLIS. *(Explaining to Stuart.)* As everything does at that age. Boys! ... *(Guiltily remembering about herself.)* And girls.

JAY. And even though a couple of them got married—let's face it, most married guys have very few male friends. And as much as men need women, they need to have other guy friends. Feel part of a—a brotherhood. So it's my job to *finally* help them get that need met.

STUART. Oh really?

JAY. In non-sexual ways.

STUART. And then suddenly they're leaping on top of every woman they can find?

PHYLLIS. *(To Stuart, warmly.)* It only takes one.

STUART. And those who can't take the—leap?

JAY. I help them accept their disorder—while firmly supporting their choice to be celibate.

STUART. You really think that's possible?!

JAY. If the little buggers have enough resolve! … "Buggers." That was accidental. But funny.

STUART. So you turn them into eunuchs.

PHYLLIS. No, he helps them concentrate on doing good deeds.

STUART. Ah. Make them all Jewish priests. That's certainly worked well for the Catholic church.

JAY. … I need some water, Phyllis.

STUART. It's on the table. Within easy reach.

PHYLLIS. No, I'll get it. *(She pours water for him, passes it to him. He takes his time and drinks.)* What's in the bag?

JAY. Nothing.

PHYLLIS. Oh come on. Show it.

(*Jay pulls out a very nice Teddy Bear.*)

STUART. (*Puzzled.*) For Phyllis?

JAY. No, Ethan.

STUART. But it's so nice.

JAY. My son doesn't deserve nice?

STUART. Of course he does. It's just that—

JAY. He'll destroy it? That's why I got it for him. He likes to pick off all of the fur.

PHYLLIS. (*Chiming in.*) And then hurl it to the ground!

JAY. While making wild noises.

(*Jay squeaks and squeals in a silly voice.*)

PHYLLIS. (*Embarrassed.*) That's enough, Jay.

JAY. It's a fun sound. A happy sound. AHHH! (*Again, Jay squeaks and squeals.*)

PHYLLIS. We'll have to wait until he's shrieked out.

JAY. (*Stops screaming.*) Oh, speaking of that! Do you know what the word for "monster" is in Yiddish?

STUART. No.

JAY. Shrek ... Like the movie. Love that. "Shrek." We just keep infiltrating American culture without them even realizing it ... And—(*Whispering a secret, demonstrating the hand salute.*)— the Vulcan salute. Leonard Nimoy based it on this gesture used by the Hebrew priests—

PHYLLIS. *(Demonstrating.)* —who separated—these fingers—to look like the letter "Shin"—

STUART. *(Bragging, he already knows all of this.)* Except the priests used both hands, stretched forward, palms down—with thumbs almost touching ... *(Close to Phyllis' hands.)* But not quite.

(A shared moment between Phyllis and Stuart. Jay is acutely aware of it.)

JAY. Let's get started. I'm starving.

PHYLLIS. You're not going to daven first?

JAY. No. We're starting.

PHYLLIS. Could we just relax for a few more— *(But Jay has already started to head off.)* Where are you going?

JAY. To get Ethan.

PHYLLIS. But he's—

STUART. *(Interrupting.)* He's with Phyllis' parents.

JAY. *He* knows this and I don't?

PHYLLIS. I'm sure I told you.

(Jay goes and now stands in front of the table. And waits. The other two realize they're supposed to join him. They do. Just as Jay sings "Shalom aleychem," Phyllis sees that he isn't wearing his yarmulke.)

PHYLLIS. Wait!

JAY. What now?

(Phyllis pats her head. Jay pulls his yarmulke out of his pocket and puts it on.)

PHYLLIS. It's strange you forgot.

(Jay sings. As they all join in, neither Phyllis nor Jay look at their prayer books. Stuart, the baltshuvah, {newly religious} uses his, intently singing the words.)

JAY. Shalom aleychem—

(Stuart and Phyllis join in.)

Malachey ha-shareyt. Malachey elyon.
Mi-melech, malchey ham'lachim. Ha-kadosh baruch hu.
Bo-akhem l'shalom. Malachey ha-shalom. Malachey elyon.
Mi-melech, malchey ham'lachim. Ha-kadosh baruch hu.

(As the song goes on, Jay sings louder until it's at the top of his lungs. And not pretty. Jay looks at no one while he belts out the song—while Stuart and Phyllis share a smile at Jay's performance. Song ends.)

STUART. When you sing, you really sing. You're like the Ethel Merman of cantors.

JAY. Actually, I've been told more like Michael Bolton…..At least he's a Jew. *(Moves on to the next song. He sings in Hebrew, quickly, at the top of his lungs, not looking at Phyllis.)*

Eyshet chayil mi yimtsa—

STUART. *(With a quiet religious conviction.)* Shouldn't you look at Phyllis during this?

JAY. What?

STUART. *(With beauty.)* You're singing "A woman of valor—her worth is more than rubies. Her husband knows he can always trust her."

JAY. I know the prayer.

STUART. You're not even looking at beautiful Phyllis.

JAY. Oh come on, I say this prayer every single week.

47

STUART. *(Almost hurt.)* And once a week is too much to thank your wife for all she's done?

(Jay's annoyed, but he knows Stuart's a baltshuvah, a bit of an earnest fanatic.)

JAY. *(To Phyllis, sings a little softer, somewhat looking at his wife.)*

Eyshet chayil mi yimtsa—

STUART. Slow down.

JAY. *(Doesn't slow down.)*

Eyshet chayil mi yimtsa—

STUART. Please. Slow down.

JAY. *(Slows down a little.)*

Eyshet chayil mi yimtsa—
V'rachok mip'ninim michra—
Batach ba leyv balah, v'shalal lo yechsar—

STUART. Shouldn't you keep looking at your wife?

JAY. G'malat-hu tov v'lo ra, kol y'mey cha-yeha. *(Turning away from Phyllis and starting to sing louder.)* Darshah tzemer u-fishtim, vata-as b'chefets kapeha.

(As Jay continues singing the song, he actually looks at his wife. His singing changes. Becomes more loving. Phyllis gets emotional watching her husband sing to her this way—something she hasn't seen in a while. Stuart becomes a little uneasy watching this.)

Tinu la mip'ri yadeha vihal'luka vash'arim ma-aseha.

PHYLLIS. I forgot what a lovely voice you can have—when you want to.

JAY. Thank you.

STUART. (Unnerved.) That was ... very moving.

JAY. (Suddenly seeing his wife.) That's a new dress, isn't it? And your hair. Is that different?

PHYLLIS. Why, yes. You noticed.

JAY. Did you do that for me ... or him?

PHYLLIS. (With a smile) Well for you ... And then him.

(Phyllis lifts the sterling Kiddish cup at her husband's place and pours the wine into it.)

JAY. (To Stuart, said perfunctorily.) Wanna make your own Kiddish or should I do it?

STUART. (Feeling uneasy after "Eyshet chayil.") You do it for me.

JAY. (Sings, still standing, says it very quickly.)

Yom has sheshee, va-ye chuluhasha-my-yeem — v'ha'ah'retz v'chol tz'vah'ahm.

Va'y'chahl Eh'lo'kim ba'yom ha'sh'vee'ee m'lach'to ah'sher ah'sah

(As Jay sings, Phyllis picks up the folded challah cover and unfolds it. Stuart and Phyllis share a look as she places the cover over the challah bread so it doesn't hear the prayer for the wine. Phyllis starts to laugh. Stuart tries to remain serious.)

JAY. What's funny?

PHYLLIS. Nothing. Keep going.

(As Jay continues praying, Phyllis and Stuart try not to laugh. Stuart gently adjusts then readjusts the bread cover to make sure the bread is truly covered — so it doesn't overhear the prayer for the wine. Phyllis and

49

Stuart laugh.)

JAY. *(As Stuart and Phyllis adjust the cover.)* Sah'v'ree mah'rah'nahn v'rah'bah'nahn v'rah'boh'tai *(The prayer for the wine.)* Baruch ata Ado-shem Elokeynu melech ha-olam, borey p'ri ha-gafen.

PHYLLIS/STUART. *(Laughing and therefore coming in a second too late)...* Amen.

(Jay sips the wine, then passes it to Phyllis. She sips and then hands it back to Jay. Then Jay holds out his Kiddish cup.)

JAY. *(Re: Stuart's glass on the table.)* Slide your cup over so I can pour into it. *(Instead, Stuart grabs Jay's Kiddish cup and drinks directly from it.)* What are you doing?!

PHYLLIS. *(To Jay.)* Why are you so upset?

JAY. Well he's ... not supposed to drink from our cup.

STUART. Who says?

JAY. It's a law.

PHYLLIS. No, it's just a tradition. I think because of sanitary reasons.

JAY. ... And now, the washing of hands. You go first, Phyllis.

PHYLLIS. But you always wash first.

JAY. Well, it obviously won't be the first tradition we've broken tonight. *(To Stuart.)* Will it, baltshuvah?

(Phyllis takes off her wedding ring and gets up to wash. She stops since they're not standing to join them.)

PHYLLIS. Aren't you coming?

JAY. Remember, no talking after you wash your hands.

PHYLLIS. You're telling me how to be a Jew? *(To Stuart.)* My family was truly religious while his was, well, perpetually looking for 'creative' ways not to be.

(Phyllis exits off, going into the kitchen.)

JAY. *(Concerned.)* What are you doing, drinking alcohol?

STUART. It was just a drop.

JAY. You shouldn't be drinking at all

STUART. I know.

JAY. You said you only visited that once—just to snoop around. Now suddenly you're my wife's lover?

STUART. What are you talking about?

JAY. The way you're flirting with her.

STUART. I do that with everyone … I didn't mean for this to happen. It's just that—well—she's SO smart—and frum. *Truly* frum. I mean sure, *you* taught me the rituals of Judaism, but *she's* helping me understand what *underlies* our rituals and laws. It's breathtaking.

JAY. If you want to learn more about Torah, go to a damn rabbi. Or hang out with a bunch of Yeshivah boys … You've invaded my home. Why are you doing this to me?

STUART. *(Confused, vulnerable.)* I don't know. I guess—I don't know. My emotions—they're so—Which I hate! … You're right. I'm acting like an idiot.

JAY. *(Touched by his confusion.)* I didn't say that, schmucko … I mean … I want to tell her.

STUART. *(Jumping to another thought.)* You can't *really* preach Same Sex Attraction Disorder … Not exactly what you were teaching *me* when *I* was your patient.

JAY. Well until I met you, I actually believed in it.

STUART. (*Touched.*) But then?

(*Phyllis reenters. Jay and Stuart quickly get up and exit the room. Phyllis looks at them puzzled, but can't speak—since you can't talk once you've washed your hands. Phyllis sits alone onstage—hears Jay say the blessing for washing of hands.*)

"*Baruch ata Ado-shem Elokeynu melech ha-olam, Asher kid'shanu b'mitsvotav, v'tsivanu al n'tilat yadayim.*"

(*She possibly hears Stuart whispering but can't make it out. Phyllis sits there, puzzled, as they fail to return to the room.*

Finally Jay reenters and without waiting for Stuart begins to say the prayers. Jay takes off the Challah cover, puts one challah next to the other, raises them and says):

JAY. Bershute. (*Translation: "With your permission." Then Jay says the "Hamozi," the blessing for the bread.*)

Baruch ata Adoshem Elokeynu melekh ha-olam, Ha-motsi lechem min ha-aretz.

(*Stuart rushes back in to be a part of the prayers.*)

PHYLLIS/STUART. Amen.

(*In silence, Jay cuts bread for all three—because he's acting as their agent. Then he takes the first piece, dips it in the salt dish, and eats it himself. Then he dips a second piece and hands it to his wife. Phyllis eats it.*)

JAY. Now Phyllis and I can talk. But you still can't. Not until you've tasted the bread.

PHYLLIS. Stuart knows the rules. (*To Stuart, concerned.*) Right? (*Stuart glares. He knows the rules. To Jay.*) Pass him the bread.

(*As Jay dips the third piece in salt, a somewhat devious thought comes over him.)*

JAY. Let's do it the Flatbush way.

PHYLLIS. I don't think that's a good—

(Jay throws a piece of bread to Stuart.)

STUART. *(As he misses catching it.)* What are you—?!

JAY/PHYLLIS. *(To Stuart.)* Shhh!

(Jay and Phyllis laugh together.)

PHYLLIS. You are bad, Jay! I'm so sorry, Stuart.

STUART. You should be!

JAY./PHYLLIS. *(To Stuart.)* Shhh!

JAY. *(Having fun, as if reprimanding a child.)* You can't talk until you've tasted the bread. *(Stuart again glares at Jay for 'instructing him.' Jay taunts him.)* Ready to try again? Maybe this time you'll catch it ... Although my sense is you were probably never that good at baseball. What did you play—right field?

PHYLLIS. Enough Jay. Just throw him the bread. *(Jay stands there, holding the bread in his hand ... as if he was about to pitch. He does the wind up. Stuart gets into position to catch it. But suddenly Jay stops.)* Come on, Jay. *(To Stuart.)* Don't worry if you don't catch it, Stuart. *(Jay throws the piece of bread. Stuart catches it. She's so relieved.)* I knew you could do it! ... I mean I wasn't a hundred percent sure, but ... I was definitely hoping. *(As Stuart eats the bread.)* Are there many gay baseball players?

JAY. Phyllis!

STUART. I'm not sure. Even if a guy's gay it's hard to tell—since ball players tend to be fairly guy-guy. You know, grabbing themselves, spitting, wearing their tight, white uniforms.

PHYLLIS. Jay loves watching the Mets play.

STUART. What do you like about the game so much?

JAY. *(Oddly personal.)* The camaraderie. The feeling of each team being almost—a brotherhood. Each of them watching the others backs … It's hard to find that.

STUART. *(Taken aback by his honesty.)* Yes….That is true. *(As they begin eating.)* I never saw anyone throw the bread—before this.

JAY. Classy families—like Phyllis'—pass the bread slices in a basket. My family thinks they're all quarterbacks or pitchers so we throw.

STUART. How'd that get started?

JAY. It's what my Dad did—and his Dad before that.

STUART. So is that a tradition or a law?

JAY. I'd say a tradition that turned into law, at least in Brooklyn.

STUART. Unlike the covering of the bread—which is a law.

JAY. Since when?

PHYLLIS. I told Stuart about the bread. Why it's supposed to be covered.

STUART. So it won't hear the blessing for the wine. Because bread is sensitive. And would be hurt if it found out it didn't get the first blessing.

JAY. Oh please, that's not why we cover the bread.

PHYLLIS. Yes it is.

JAY. No, it's just a family tradition.

PHYLLIS. No, it's a law.

JAY. I am sure you're wrong—

PHYLLIS. Jay, don't even *try* arguing Torah with me. We both know who always wins. Don't we?

JAY. … Who even knew our bread was sensitive? The only thing in our family that is! *(Intrigued.)* So *that's* why we cover it.

STUART. The way you sang "Woman of Valor". It made me remember how my grandfather sang it to my grandmother. Grinning the whole time.

JAY. My Dad raced through it. Grandpa did the same thing. *(Surprised.)* … It felt good to sing it differently.

STUART. So it doesn't always have to be the way your father did it—and his father did it?

JAY. Maybe not.

(Jay gets quiet. Lost in his own thoughts.)

PHYLLIS. *(To Jay,)* Almost made me cry when you sang it … *(Back to her determination to make Ethan normal.)* Did I tell both of you that Ethan picked which hand had the shoe and the fork eight times out of ten. Eight times out of ten! I've read on the internet about children suddenly making huge improvements. I'm sure you've seen that happen yourself.

STUART. I wish I could say I have—

PHYLLIS. *(Not wanting to hear.)* Oh, well, I certainly don't want you to lie to me. I wouldn't want that.

STUART. And I wouldn't lie to you, Phyllis. I wouldn't—*(Realizing he has.)*— lie.

(During the following conversation, Stuart now gets silent, contemplative.)

PHYLLIS. *(Seeing Jay also in his own thoughts.)* Are you all right?

JAY. Just quiet.

PHYLLIS. Which is hardly like you.

JAY. The three of us sitting here—you know—it really IS ... something.

PHYLLIS. It's just three Jews hanging out on Shabbos.

JAY. ...Exactly. Exchanging ideas. Learning a few things about the world.

STUART. *(Half to himself, finally realizing what's he done.)* About ourselves.

PHYLLIS. Yes, of course.

JAY. And that really *is* something. Here we are truly enjoying the quiet beauty of Shabbos—which is basically the heart of Judaism. Do you see?

PHYLLIS. ...I think so. *(Sensing something is going on.)* Pass the bread.

STUART. *(Realizing he shouldn't be there.)* You're right, Jay. Shabbos is where it all begins.

JAY. Completely ... Stuart understands.

PHYLLIS. And so do I.

JAY. We're taking time from running around—to find one day we're with those ... we love. Home. Hearth.

STUART. This is a sacred day.

JAY. Exactly. Sacred. Holy. All that stuff. Good stuff.

STUART. Holiness. *(Half to himself.)* So what am I doing?

JAY. What?

PHYLLIS. What every good Jew is supposed to be doing. Honoring the Shabbos bride.

(They all eat some more. Stuart continues to take in his inappropriate actions. Then finally.)

STUART. I just remembered, I uh—have rounds tonight. I have to go. I'm so sorry, Phyllis.

PHYLLIS. Rounds? On Shabbos?

STUART. A doctor is exempt from Shabbos rules—if there's the possibility of saving a life.

PHYLLIS. Of course. It's just that you didn't mention that you had rounds—

JAY. *(Completely thrown.)* You haven't even finished your dinner.

STUART. *(To Phyllis.)* The hospital is in walking distance. I won't be driving.

PHYLLIS. I didn't think you would be.

STUART. *(To Phyllis, blurting out.)* You should be spending Shabbos with—the "right" people.

PHYLLIS. The right people?

STUART. Thank you, Phyllis. And Jay? *(Jay is momentarily too stunned to speak.)* ... Jay?

JAY. Uh ... Yes, Stuart?

STUART. It was nice meeting you.

JAY. (Confused.) Yes. Yes … And hopefully we'll celebrate another Shabbos soon.

STUART. (Breaking up with Jay.) With my crazy schedule, it's sort of—unlikely.

(Stuart finally stands and begins to exit. Jay is stunned.)

PHYLLIS. But I specially cooked this meal for you. I mean I cooked it for Jay as well—(A little embarrassed she admitted that.) It's not as if you can pick up dinner now. It's already Shabbos—

JAY. (Finishing sentence.) —so you can't spend money. Might as well stay here and have dinner. That's what you should do.

(The Phone begins to ring.)

STUART. (Pointed.) I'll be perfectly fine—on my own.

JAY. Stuart! Stuart!

STUART. … What?

JAY. (Thinking fast.) Uh—It's so strange! The phone! Everyone knows we can't answer the phone on Shabbos. And still, look! It's ringing.

STUART. It's probably just a telemarketer.

JAY. No, we're on the "do not call" list.

STUART. Phyllis, accept my apologies—for leaving so soon.

(Stuart starts to go again.)

JAY. (Trying to stop Stuart from leaving.) I know this sounds crazy, but Stuart!—Stuart!—for some reason I feel the urge to answer it! The phone!

STUART. Fight it.

JAY. *(Flipping out.)* But if this were the only call I answered, my only sin, would it really be so terrible?! What if I suddenly decide from now on to use the phone on Shabbos, but in *all* other ways keep it holy?! Does that one little sin negate all of my reverence?!

STUART. It's more than a *little* sin.

(Phone stops ringing.)

JAY. I know, but I want to pick up the phone, Stuart ... I want to pick up the phone and talk.

PHYLLIS. Why?

JAY. *(From his heart.)* Because ... it's what I feel.

PHYLLIS. *(Knows something strange is going on.)* What you feel? Sit down and stop talking crazy.

JAY. It's only crazy to you! Not to me. Or to Stuart! Right Stuart? ... Right, Stuart?

STUART. *(Doesn't want this scene to happen this way.)* Jay ... Please ...

PHYLLIS. ... The two of you know each other? Jay? *(But he's lost in his own drama.)* Stuart?

JAY. But how can something be a sin when it feels so honest and—How?

PHYLLIS. *(Beginning to realize, but not wanting to believe it.)* Oh my god.

JAY. The three of us were just talking. So warmly. Sharing Shabbos. *(Going to Stuart.)* Our first Shabbos.

PHYLLIS. *(Disbelieving)* No.

JAY. It felt so beautiful. And then the ringing.

PHYLLIS. *(Firmly.)* No.

(Fast blackout as Stuart and Jay exit. Then lights swiftly back up on

… Phyllis. She stands there, enraged. Then grabs one of the place settings and takes it offstage. The phone begins to ring. She reenters. Knows it's Jay. Wants to answer it. But then stops herself. She looks around the room. Stares at the crazy colored carpet which Jay loves. She takes the rug, rolls it up and exits offstage as …

Jay reenters. And although he stands in this room, he is actually no longer in his and Phyllis' apartment.

From now on, Jay's life's divided in two. There's his old life and apartment with Phyllis and his new life and apartment with Stuart. Perhaps there was even an upstage flat that has now been split open to show that. And yet, while Jay goes back and forth between two apartments, on this stage the two apartments occupy the same space. So the one table is used for both apartments.

Jay takes out his cell phone and calls his home phone again. It begins to ring. Phyllis reenters — looks at the ringing phone, is tempted once again, then finally doesn't answer it and leaves.

During this, Jay drops his suit jacket on the floor (in Stuart's apartment) and exits just as Stuart reenters and sees Jay's jacket on the floor. Though a little annoyed, Stuart still picks up Jay's jacket and hangs it on a second hook on the wall and exits. {The first hook still has Jay's coat of many colors hanging on it — which is in Phyllis' apartment.}

Then lights shift to another evening. A Friday evening. Phyllis enters, carrying in two Shabbos candles. Places them next to the phone. She takes out a white lace kerchief and places it on her head.

While at the same time, Stuart and Jay enter. They take two of the chairs and move them far downstage and sit. These chairs are used to represent subway seats.

During the above, Phyllis lights the Sabbath candles. She hesitates lighting the second candle (since it's represents the marriage union), but finally she does light them both. Then makes three circles above the candles with her hands, covers her eyes and says the blessing over the lighting of the candles.)

PHYLLIS.
Baruch ata ado-shem elokeynu melech ha-olam
asher kid'shanu b'mitzvotav— *(Phyllis stops, trying not to cry. But then continues.)*
v'tsivanu, le-hadlik ner, shel Shabbat.

(Phyllis begins to wander around her apartment. Upset. Glaring at the walls. While at the same time:

Jay and Stuart are on a subway car. Stuart publicly wears a yarmulke as he grows more religious. He reads a book listing the 613 commandments. Jay does not wear his yarmulke.

Jay's legs are sprawled out, not to be affectionate, but because he's simply taking up too much space. The subway car isn't moving.)

STUART. This is one of my fantasies.

JAY. *(Titillated.)* Doing it on the subway?

STUART. The two of us heading home together for our first Shabbos … I don't think we're going to make it.

JAY. Of course we will.

STUART. Not if the subway doesn't start moving soon.

JAY. Well that's a relief. I thought you meant us. Not making it.

(Phyllis exits—with a plan in mind.)

STUART. We should have left work earlier. If we're not home by sunset, we are being disrespectful—

JAY. We're just a couple stops from your apartment. We'll be there soon … Kind of thrilling, don't you think? The drama of it all. Wondering—"will we beat the sun? Make it home on time for Shabbos?"

STUART. That's sacrilegious.

JAY. Excuse me, but just last week, who was making fun of the bread?

STUART. And I apologize for that.

JAY. Don't.

(PHYLLIS. reenters, carrying in a bucket of water and a brush. Although knowing she's prohibited from writing or erasing on Shabbos, she still begins scrubbing off crayons and paint from her apartment wall as Jay looks at this subway "walls.")

JAY. I remember when these subway walls were covered in graffiti— inside and out! Now look at them. They're almost blindingly bright.

STUART. It *is* great.

JAY. No it's not, schmucko. Not in New York!

STUART. (*Amused.*) Oh, okay. It's not great.

JAY. How did those graffiti artists do it? Hurling all their rage, love, frustration onto a wall. To be able to just throw your feelings right out there. In front of everyone. Hey! Maybe that's how G-d created the world. Maybe *he* was actually the first graffiti artist. (*Pretending to be G-d, splashing colors.*) Splash. Heavens … Splash. Earth … Huh. It *is* good.

STUART. (*Amused*) You and Phyllis. Where do you guys come up with your crazy theories?

JAY. I still can't believe she kicked me out. And that I let her. Why did I do that?

STUART. To be with someone you loved.

JAY. *(Warmly)* Of course.

STUART. I hope she's okay. I've thought about calling her, but—She doesn't want to talk to me anyway … Are you playing leggsies with me?

JAY. I'm just enjoying the G-d-given space between my legs.

STUART. Well, it's cramping me. So tell G-d to give you a little less space down there. *(Jay shifts to make room as Stuart checks his watch again.)* Sunset—thirty minutes and counting.

JAY. *(Calling out to Conductor.)* Hey, is anyone working?! Some of us need to get moving!

STUART. *(Surprised.)* You did that for me?

JAY. *(To Stuart.)* Actually, my claustrophobia kicked in a few minutes ago.

STUART. You never told me you were claustrophobic.

JAY. There are some things you wait to bring up until you get closer.

STUART. It still amazes me you're a therapist.

JAY. Oh and speaking of that—your tie—I hate the way you tie it.

STUART. This is a classic Windsor knot.

JAY. Hate it … Claustrophobia … getting stronger.

STUART. We'll be moving soon.

JAY. I will NOT die on this subway. Got too much to live for … *(Lovingly to Stuart.)* especially now, schmucko.

STUART. You are incredibly bizarre. But sometimes you say exactly the right thing.

(Stuart continues reading.

Phyllis continues scrubbing the walls. Although Jay doesn't see her, he feels her presence.)

JAY. *(Thinking, to himself.)* Maybe I should move back with Phyllis.

STUART. Why?

JAY. To see Ethan. She's got no right to keep me from him. I should have just said: "No, I'm not leaving!" But she was so ... *(Surprised.)* strong.

STUART. At this moment, she doesn't need to be stuck living with a gay husband.

JAY. Voice down. *(Stuart looks puzzled.)* The word "gay"!

STUART. What does it matter? By now the whole congregation must know you've moved in with me.

JAY. How? We don't even sit together at synagogue. Although hold on—they *have* seen me talk to you. Oh god.

(Phyllis exits offstage.)

STUART. What?

JAY. I just remembered some of them pointing at you. One guy called you "The Frum Fagella!"

STUART. And what did you say to defend me?

JAY. I thought it was an interesting alliteration.

STUART. Well they got it wrong. I'm gay—like it or not. Being frum—being orthodox—is what I choose—what I truly am. So I'm not the Frum Fagella. I'm the Fagella Frum. And now, so are you!

JAY. Hardly. The synagogue doesn't know for sure. Me, they'll give the benefit of the doubt.

STUART. Because?

JAY. I'm masculine.

STUART. Excuse me?

JAY. I'm the frum from birth! One of them. Also, Phyllis's family have been part of the shul for generations. It gives me a certain position. I mean I get an Aliyah almost every week.

STUART. You're lucky. Being Orthodox, you've always belonged to a — a real community. I never felt comfortable with my wishy-washy conservative Jewish upbringing — where you pick and choose which rules you want to follow — ignore the rest. For me, Judaism must be a living, binding, demanding religion or what's the point?

JAY. I love it when you're judgmental.

(Stuart then begins reading from his booklet some more as Jay anxiously waits for the subway to get going.)

STUART. *(To Jay, pointed.)* Ah hah. Commandment one hundred eight. Not to travel on Shabbat outside the limits of one's place of residence —

(Suddenly we hear the sound of the subway car moving again.)

JAY. Finally — we're moving.

(Without thinking, Jay puts his hand on top of Stuart's hand.)

STUART. *(Surprised to see Jay's hand on top of his.)* Your hand.

JAY. *(Examining it.)* Look at that. Without even thinking — It feels nice. Should I keep it there?

STUART. You're joking … Right? … You're the one who's always been uncomfortable touching.

JAY. Because I was married.

STUART. You always say when you see two men holding hands, you feel like they're about to go skipping down the street.

JAY. Well it *does* look that way … when *other* guys are doing it. *(Still holding Stuart's hand.)* I guess it does with us, too. *(Beat.)* I don't want to let go.

STUART. Then keep holding.

(Jay does for a moment and then finally—after much internal struggle—lets go.)

JAY. That's all I can do.

STUART. It's a start.

JAY. *(Pleased.)* … Who would have thought, here, in our pristine subway—suddenly a splash of color—*(Pleased/surprised.)*—from me.

(Phyllis reenters, bringing in a suitcase and a handful of Jay's clothes. She begins angrily stuffing the suitcase with clothes while at the same time:

Jay and Stuart walk into another area which represents Stuart's dining area. Jay is there first.)

JAY. Where are your candles?

STUART. *(Entering, stunned.)* You can't light them now. Shabbos has already started.

JAY. I know, but—

STUART. That goes against one of the 613 commandments.

JAY. I like seeing the candles lit. It's comforting. It's just a little sin. I'm already sinning being with you … And if you hadn't been late, we would have been able to light them.

STUART. *Both* of us were late. Because of you!

JAY. Wrong. Since this is *your* home, you're the host. And the host is always the one who is responsible—*(Not wanting to deal with all that.)* Forget it. *(Sings.)* Shalom Aleychem—

STUART. What are you doing?

JAY. Starting.

STUART. The host is supposed to start.

JAY. I *always* lead.

STUART. *(Re: something sexual.)* The other night? *(sings)* Shalom aleychem—

JAY. Whoa there!

(But Stuart keeps singing. Jay, somewhat amused, jumps in, singing with him.)

STUART/JAY.

Malachey ha-shareyt. Malachey elyon.

(As they sing, the stress of the day begins to lessen. We see the affection the men have for each other as the song progresses.)

Mi-melech, malachey ham'lachim. Ha-kadosh baruch hu.

(While on the other side of the stage, Phyllis has brought in more clothes and continues to angrily stuff them into a suitcase as she angrily sings. Phyllis on one side, Stuart and Jay on the other. All sing.)

Bo-achem l'shalom. Malachey ha-shalom. Malachey elyon.

Mi-melech, malachey ham'lachim. Ha-kadosh baruch hu.

(Song ends. Jay doesn't move on to the next prayer.)

STUART. What?

JAY. … I'm so used to hearing a male and female voice on Shabbos.

STUART. I think our two voices are a fun sound. A happy sound.

JAY. (Getting the reference to his son, amused.) … I'm not disagreeing.

(Jay and Stuart look back down at the prayer book and then each starts to sing "A Woman of Valor.")

JAY/STUART. Eyshet chayil mi yimtsa—

(They both stop, realizing they have another religious dilemma.)

PHYLLIS. (In her space, sings, angrily remembering how Jay sang it to her.) —chayil mi yimtsa

JAY. (To Stuart.) We both can't sing "A Woman of Valor."

STUART. I want you to know that I value you.

JAY. And vice versa … One of us has to be the woman.

(Stalemate.)

PHYLLIS. (Continues singing to herself, a growing annoyance with Jay.) v'rakhok mip'ninim mikhra

JAY. We could skip it.

STUART. (Thinking it through.) We're required to sing it.

JAY. You do the cooking so it kinda makes sense for me to sing "A Woman of Valor"—to you.

STUART. I'm a doctor.

JAY. I'm a psychologist.

STUART. *(He's won.)* So there *you* have it! A medical doctor trumps a— *(Off Jay's indignant glare.)* Let's both do it. We both value each other, right?

JAY. Right.

STUART. So, ready and—

JAY. *(Jumping in ahead of Stuart.)*

Eyshet chayil mi yimtsa!

STUART/JAY. *(singing)*

v'rakhok mip'ninim mikhra—

(Phyllis also sings, but enraged. She sees Jay's coat of many colors, grabs it and exits as Jay and Stuart sing warmly to each other.)

Batakh ba leyv balah, v'shalal lo yekhsar—
G'malat-hu tov v'lo ra, kol y'mey kha-yeha.

STUART. Fix my tie.

STUART/JAY. *(As Jay begins to undo Stuart's tie.)*

Darshah tsemer u-fishtim, vata-as b'khafets kapeha.
Tinu la mip'ri yadeha vihal'luka — bash'arim ma-aseha.

(As they finish the prayer, lights fade on Jay and Stuart and perhaps a hipper recorded version of "Eyshet Chayil" is heard. As they exit, Phyllis reenters carrying in Jay's suitcase. It's two days later.

Sunday afternoon. In Phyllis and Jay's apartment. Ethan's laughing offstage in the other room. Jay laughs with him. Phyllis onstage is annoyed.)

JAY. *(Enters.)* Who's the guy?

PHYLLIS. A grad student in psychology at Columbia. His name is Jimmy.

JAY. Since when do you pick a tutor without me?

PHYLLIS. Since I needed a lot more help these days.

JAY. If you let me back in, you wouldn't. *(Silence.)* And why is he here now? This is when I take Ethan swimming.

PHYLLIS. Today he's working on fork and shoe instead.

JAY. He loves swimming.

PHYLLIS. I should have changed the locks. And I'm going to. You can't just barge into my apartment.

JAY. Until last week it was our apartment. You can't cut me out. And I need my clothes—

PHYLLIS. They're in the suitcase.

JAY. I've got a helluva lot more than that.

PHYLLIS. *(Puzzled.)* You don't even look gay. I mean you're not even that handsome.

JAY. *(Looking into suitcase)* … I think I need some water.

PHYLLIS. At least Stuart looks gay.

JAY. You didn't think so originally—from what he told me.

PHYLLIS. Well—he was so good looking—it took me a while to concentrate—really hear him. See his mannerisms.

JAY. *(Realizing.)* I knew they were bad!

PHYLLIS. Why should you care? You're in his camp.

JAY. I could really use some water.

PHYLLIS. So do I seem overtly male? Is that why you—

JAY. No.

PHYLLIS. Although in comparison to Stuart, I suppose I am.

JAY. You can't *really* think Stuart's more handsome than me?

PHYLLIS. Say it once more and I won't ask again.

JAY. I'm sure. Where's my coat?

PHYLLIS. No, say the word gay. Not yes or I'm sure.

JAY. I've already said that's what I am.

PHYLLIS. All right. Well now that I definitely know, I want you out.

JAY. *(Amused.)* You've already kicked me out of our home!

PHYLLIS. *(Dead serious.)* But now the entire neighborhood. *(Getting idea.)* Actually all of Manhattan. To Queens.

JAY. You're telling me where to go. And to Queens no less.

PHYLLIS. There's a large Orthodox population there—none of whom I know. So you can become friendly with them. If they'll befriend you.

JAY. My practice is here on the Upper West Side, our synagogue. Our friends.

PHYLLIS. As well as my parents—who are disgraced.

JAY. You told them?!

PHYLLIS. Oddly, my father wasn't that surprised.

JAY. You're lying.

PHYLLIS. I'm not the liar here.

JAY. You're just being vindictive. I feel sorry—

PHYLLIS. You never tried hitting on my father, did you?

JAY. I'm gay, not blind!

PHYLLIS. Well finally you said it. You actually said you were gay.

JAY. Happy?

PHYLLIS. I had no idea you were so proud of being—

JAY. I'm not proud. *You're* forcing me to be. And speaking of forcing, you've got to stop making Ethan do fork and shoe all the time.

PHYLLIS. And the reason?

JAY. Because he can't learn it. And it upsets him. You've been trying to drill it into him for the past 3 years. Let him be a happy child and learn at his own pace.

PHYLLIS. *(Honest.)* He doesn't have a pace.

JAY. Yet.

PHYLLIS. He'll never have one if we don't push him.

JAY. Then we'll have to accept that.

PHYLLIS. *(She won't.)* … I want you out of our community. I'm not in the mood for other frummies pointing at you, laughing. Pointing at me—feeling sorry for me again.

JAY. *(Enraged—doesn't like Phyllis being picked on.)* Is that what they're doing to you?!

PHYLLIS. They will. Poor Phyllis. Crazy son. Homosexual husband. Could G-d spare her no indignity?

JAY. Our son is not crazy. Who said that to you? I'll punch him in the nose.

PHYLLIS. It wasn't said — in words. But the way the ladies at shul look at me — with such sympathy — I could spit.

JAY. You should!

PHYLLIS. Well ... I should. But instead, you're moving to Queens.

JAY. Stop saying that. I'm a Manhattanite.

PHYLLIS. Even the Gomorrah says if you must go to a prostitute, go to one in another town. Don't bring shame on your community. If you remembered your Talmud, you'd know the concept of public shame AND the dignity in keeping things private.

JAY. *(Changing subject.)* Your father *had* to be stunned I was gay. I mean come on — look at me.

PHYLLIS. *(Ignoring that.)* Right now, other people only suspect. But if I confirmed the rumor —

JAY. Please, that's not you. You're not that cruel. Why am I so thirsty? Phyllis, I need some water.

PHYLLIS. *(Cold.)* The rage I've felt — I didn't even know I had it in me.

JAY. I still don't see you telling the congregation. You wouldn't want the public shame.

PHYLLIS. I'd hate it. My only consolation: it would be worse for you. How would you be treated? How many Aliyahs would you have then? Most of your patients are orthodox. How many would

73

keep seeing you?

JAY. Are you threatening me?

PHYLLIS. You mean by telling the truth?! *(Back to the previous thought.)* Oh and *especially* — especially the ones you've been teaching reparative therapy to! … Maybe you should have tried it on yourself! *(No answer.)* Did you — try it? *(He's not giving anything away. Which pisses her off.)* I've already cleaned out the apartment of your presence. Same as sweeping, then burning the unwanted bread before Passover. Now I want your presence gone from the entire borough. Yes.

JAY. I already told you I am not—

PHYLLIS. And why did you really wear that coat? Was it some kind of code for other men to tell that—

JAY. You're talking like a wacko. You know Ethan made it for me.

PHYLLIS. Yes, and *not* for me. I suppose for some reason, he thinks you have more of the maternal instinct. Well at least now I understand why.

JAY. I am not remotely maternal and you know it. Who knows why he gave me that coat!

PHYLLIS. Because you love him unconditionally. Now it makes sense. One freak loving the other!

(Silence.)

JAY. Where's my coat?

PHYLLIS. In the spare room.

(Jay goes offstage. Phyllis calls out — upset at what she said about her son.)

PHYLLIS. I love Ethan! *(Jay reenters, holding up his Coat of Many*

Colors. Except it is now just a plain looking trench coat. All the colors have been bleached out. Jay is enraged.) See, I *am* that cruel … I took it to the dry cleaners and—

JAY. *(Furious, but somewhat keeping it in.)* Did Ethan see this?

PHYLLIS. He won't notice it's missing.

JAY. On some level, I think he will.

PHYLLIS. So you want to come back? You did just mention it … And if Stuart hadn't showed up, we'd still be together. So obviously the marriage was working. Is it just sex you need from a man?

JAY. This isn't easy to talk about.

PHYLLIS. You're the therapist. Do it! … I can't figure it out. I mean you and I made love only a couple of days before you left.

JAY. I'm a horny guy.

PHYLLIS. I know. And I've never complained. *(Moving closer.)* I liked it.

JAY. So did I.

PHYLLIS. *(Embarrassed, maybe even wanting the sex right now.)* Sometimes when I felt stressed after a long day with Ethan, it was helpful. The sex. I mean it was enjoyable as well. And I was glad it was with you. But…it was helpful. *(There's a pounding from below.)* We're not even making noise and that Ukrainian bitch—!!

JAY. … Go ahead. Ask your questions.

PHYLLIS. *(She isn't quite ready to ask the really personal ones.)* How can you even be with a man and say the prayers?

JAY. In my mind, Stuart is here. Prayers, there. Never mix. Never worry.

PHYLLIS. You can compartmentalize your life that easily?

JAY. I have no choice! If I let one of my worlds encroach on the other, my head would explode! Which of course is what it's doing now. Only a couple of years ago did I even tell my shrink! I kept hoping if I didn't actually say it out loud, it wasn't real ... (*Finally admitting.*) And I tried reparative therapy. I kept thinking it was working, but then ... Failure ... I *should've* told you. But if I did, I knew I'd lose you and Judaism. And Ethan.

PHYLLIS. So when did you actually know you liked men? ... In the middle of our marriage? (*Jay is silent—he won't answer these questions.*) Before? (*Jay is silent.*) Was Stuart the first? ... I'm sure he wasn't. You wouldn't risk everything for the first guy you met. You'd wait for the one that really meant something. (*Jay is silent.*) Right?

JAY. (*The only answer he'll give.*) I was always safe. Extremely safe.

PHYLLIS. (*Stunned*) ... How long have you known Stuart?

JAY. About six months.

(*Phyllis takes that in. It's not easy to hear.*)

PHYLLIS. Why did he pretend he was looking for a caterer?

JAY. I guess he wanted to meet you. You'd have to ask him.

PHYLLIS. He won't return my calls.

JAY. You've called *him* and you haven't called *me?!*

PHYLLIS. Why did he show up for Shabbos dinner when he knew you'd be there?

JAY. To confront me? I don't know.

PHYLLIS. You never asked?

JAY. To what end?

PHYLLIS. To get closer to the truth! Supposedly that's what we're striving for in life. It just doesn't seem like something he'd do. He was a curse ... And a godsend. Helping Ethan. Making me feel ... well ...

JAY. Sexy?

PHYLLIS. Well yes. Sexy. And don't you dare tell me you're jealous of that! (*Lashing out.*) Also, I hope you know that your 'relationship' with Stuart will NEVER last!

JAY. Excuse me?

PHYLLIS. You've been spoiled by Judaism. Being in charge. Being waited upon.

JAY. You didn't wait on me.

PHYLLIS. Oh Jay! ... You didn't notice because you'd gotten used to it. Don't worry. I had no problem with that. I like being needed. Even if someone else doesn't realize it. (*Dawning on her.*) Maybe that's why G-d sent me Ethan ... But unlike me, Stuart's a busy doctor—who needs someone to be compassionate to *him*. And that's not in your vocabulary.

JAY. (*Taking that in.*) Are these your questions?

PHYLLIS. (*Continuing on.*) You can't help it. You're oblivious to other's needs. Like the way you spread your legs when we're sitting together, taking up two thirds of the space. Or when I start to order at a restaurant and you interrupt—ordering ahead of me. Or you saying you're thirsty—three times today—expecting me to get you the water. Which isn't happening anymore, "schmucko." And of course—your satisfactory—but limited performance in bed.

JAY. That's enough.

PHYLLIS. People always say Jews make the best lovers. They have GOT to be referring to Conservative and Reform!

JAY. … This discussion is over.

PHYLLIS. Whenever it's criticizing you, discussion over. I doubt Stuart will be as easy going. I think you're finally getting your just rewards—forced to live with another man! … Although isn't it ironic? You're the one who ended up with a doctor.

JAY. … I'll be back another time—when you become sane again.

PHYLLIS. Do you do that silly little dance for him when you brush your teeth?

JAY. No. I only did that with you.

PHYLLIS. That's nice to know. And do you—

(*Suddenly there is a scream from the other room. It's Ethan's voice.*)

ETHAN (*Offstage.*) AHHH!

(*As Ethan continues screaming, Jay starts to race towards Ethan's room as Phyllis starts to get a bag of cookies from the kitchen area. Jay sees this.*)

JAY. (*Enraged*) Don't, Phyllis! (*She has the cookies in her hand by now.*) Don't!!

PHYLLIS. The cookies will work!

JAY. No! … No.

PHYLLIS. Fine.

(*As the screaming continues with an offstage Ethan, Jay races to his son. Phyllis stands there a moment.*

On another part of the stage a slightly nervous Stuart enters with a shopping bag. He takes out a box. Looks around, making sure that Jay isn't around. Clearly there's something in it that he doesn't want Jay to see. Stuart opens it. And takes out—Tzitzis—a religious undergarment with fringes. Also known as tallit katan. He admires it. Then takes off his own shirt and reverentially puts on the tallit katan—for the first time. It feels a little odd. But oddly right. At the same time ...

Back in Phyllis and Jay's Old Apartment. Phyllis hears an offstage Jay singing to their son.)

JAY. *(Offstage, sings.)*

THOUGH THE RAIN IS POURING
THOUGH THE WIND IS STRONG
BABY KEEP ON SLEEPIN'
ALL NIGHT LONG

(Phyllis stands by the door and listens to her ex-husband sing. Ethan's screams decrease. Phyllis realizes that at least this man will be there for their son.)

JAY.

MAMA'S HERE BESIDE YOU
DADDY'S NEXT TO HER
BABY KEEP ON SLEEPIN'
AS YOU WERE—AS YOU WERE

(Ethan has grown quiet. Tranquil. Other side of the stage, Stuart grows tranquil as he wears his tallit katan. He begins to silently shuckle and pray while ... Back with Phyllis and Jay.)

JAY. *(Offstage, about to head back in, talking to Jimmy)* You're sure? ... All right, then. *(Jay comes back onstage, to Phyllis.)* We should give Jimmy a chance to take care of things now. Giving Ethan cookies— the easy way out.

PHYLLIS. It always works.

JAY. AND, he's putting on weight.

PHYLLIS. Is Jimmy okay?

JAY. He's trained to deal with these things.

PHYLLIS. From now on, only boys should take care of Ethan.

JAY. Why?

PHYLLIS. He's getting stronger.

JAY. No, he's not.

PHYLLIS. He scratched me quite a bit the other day. And this time it was harder to fight back.

(Phyllis shows a part of her arm that until then had been covered.)

JAY. (reacting) Are you okay?

PHYLLIS. No ... I hate that he's getting stronger. Someday he's going to hurt someone and we'll have to put him away.

JAY. (Enraged.) That is not remotely an option. ... From now on, he should live half of the time with me—

PHYLLIS. (Not pleased.) Oh is that what you think?! Now THAT is not remotely an option.

JAY. Don't answer now. Just think about it.

PHYLLIS. There's nothing to think about ... If anyone ever told me this would be my—An autistic son—

JAY. And a fagella freak husband.

PHYLLIS. Exactly ... It's certainly never dull ... You sure Ethan didn't hurt Jimmy?

JAY. Are you kidding?! Jimmy is six foot four—built like Goliath. Ethan's autistic—not stupid! (Both laugh.) I'm here for you. And Ethan. (Sings.)

MAMA'S HERE BESIDE YOU
DADDY'S NEXT TO HER

BABY KEEP ON SLEEPING
AS YOU WERE. AS YOU WERE

(Jay lightly kisses Phyllis on the head. She pulls away. Then allows it. While at the same time, Stuart takes the tzitzis and lovingly kisses them. Lights fade on Jay and Phyllis (who exit.)

But remain on Stuart. He tucks in his shirt. Then takes out a tie, puts it around his neck and looks at the tie. And to the tzitzis. Then looks back at the tie as lights come up on...

Stuart and Jay's apartment. Weeks later. Jay, offstage, and Stuart speak in a shorthand that only comes with a certain amount of solid and earned familiarity.)

JAY. *(Calling from offstage.)* I still can't get over it! *(Making himself laugh.)* I mean even today!

STUART. My tie.

JAY. *(Offstage.)* Two months ago, Miguel Abramowitz—from the Y.M.H.A.—asked if I'd give a lecture—

STUART. *(Amused.)* I already know this story, Jay.

JAY. *(Offstage.)* I replied, "Sure, but only if *I* get to pick the topic!" The look on Miguel's face: stunned. Still cracks me up!

STUART. *(Amused.)* Obviously, he didn't know you.

JAY. *(Offstage.)* Oh and I think Miguel is one of us.

STUART. *(Dryly.)* Jewish? That's surprising for a guy working at the Y.M.H.A.

JAY. No, gay! .... *(Enters, dressed for work.)* Or was that a joke? *(Stuart grins. Jay starts to head out.)* Text me later and we'll figure out dinner.

STUART. Not so fast. The tie.

JAY. I've got an eight a.m.—

STUART. And I want it looking good, so no rushing. (*Jay gets behind Stuart and begins to tie his tie.*) How could you leave without tying my tie?

JAY. I wasn't thinking?

STUART. Work is important. But the tie ceremony—*your* idea—is equally important.

JAY. Even if I'm late and lose a patient?

STUART. I could be late for morning services, but you don't see *me* rushing … (*Considers, concerned.*) Although maybe we *should* skip the tie. I like the guys knowing I'm reliable.

JAY. You've been going every morning for months. To them, you're as regular as prunes. If anything, don't show up on time.

STUART. Because?

JAY. (*Mysteriously*) Something will happen.

STUART. Yeah, they'll be annoyed with me.

JAY. Please, everything annoys *them.*

STUART. I *like* talking to the altercockers.

JAY. Arguing politics? Obama? Israel?

STUART. We try to stick to Judaism. This last month, we've been discussing *Moreh Nebukim*. (*Jay is silent.*) *Guide for the Perplexed.*

JAY. (*Surprised.*) No, I know it's—Wow. I always meant to study it, but….*Guide for the Perplexed.* I'm impressed … You never told me you were reading it.

STUART. (*Jokingly.*) Are you jealous?

JAY. Do I have reason to be? *(Beat. Then Jay and Stuart both laugh. Then Jay continues to work on the tie.)* I finally figured out my talk at the Y.M.H.A. 'Anxiety'. What Jew can't relate to anxiety?

STUART. Sounds like a hit.

JAY. Yesterday, Miguel asked if I was married. For my bio. I said "separated." He said "Oh, the women in class will be glad to hear that." I wanted to tell him — "sorry to disappoint the ladies, but I'm off the market. See I'm with this guy — who makes me feel — so many damn ... colors."

STUART. *(Touched.)* I know.

JAY. *(Puzzled.)* In my head, I said that to Miguel. But I couldn't say it out loud. I don't know why damnit! And Stuart, I want to apologize for that.

STUART. You don't need to.

JAY. *(Perplexed.)* Yeah, I do. How come I couldn't say it?

STUART. Honestly, you don't need to announce our relationship to the world.

JAY. Don't kid me. You're the one who wants to be open, but discreet. Which I completely get.

STUART. ... You don't need to announce our relationship to the world.

(Jay is puzzled by that statement.)

JAY. *(Re: the tie.)* Hold still.

STUART. *(About something other than the tie.)* I'm trying, Jay ... I'm really trying.

(Jay finishes the tie by now and inspects Stuart.)

JAY. Looks good. How does it feel?

STUART. Still tighter. You know I like it a little constricting.

JAY. (*As he tightens.*) I know. But there's a fine line and then suddenly—

STUART. Can't breathe!

JAY. (*As he loosens the tie.*) So what time will you be home?

STUART. Seven at the latest. Chinese?

JAY. Shanghai Shecky's it is. (*Re: finishing tying the tie.*) Perfect. Interesting how a tie is close to the heart.

STUART. (*Tenderly*) Almost touching. (*Beat. They share the silence. Then Stuart warmly says.*) Same as this tefillin box *almost* touches the heart.

JAY. And also constricts—just like the tie.

STUART. (*Holding up leather tefillin straps.*) Not *just* constricts. Binds. Lovingly. In the Mishhah, Maimonides says it's an intimate reminder that we must dedicate our physical, emotional and intellectual capacity to god's service. Our rebbe confessed that it's more intimate and sensual than holding his wife. Of course he's been married for 28 years.

JAY. And that's what we have to look forward to?

STUART. I hope so … 28 years.

JAY. … You're studying the Mishnah?

STUART. I'm trying. The more I read, the more I see what sinners we are.

JAY. (*Casually.*) Everyone is.

STUART. No. I'm talking about you and me—what sinners we are—being together ... Just by being together, Jay.

(Silence.)

JAY. *(Concerned, anxious.)* Well, sure. I felt the same way. Which is why it took me so long to come out ... How long have you felt this way?

STUART. ... Don't worry. I'm still wearing your tie close to my heart. *(Beat.)* I need some coffee. *(Jay, now in the role that Phyllis played, walks off to get Stuart's coffee as an uneasy Stuart continues dressing for work. Jay reenters with coffee tray. Stuart takes coffee. Jay pours his milk until Stuart nods and says.)* When.

JAY. *(As Jay stops pouring.)* Now. *(Off Stuart's puzzlement.)* All we have, Stuart. Now.

STUART. *(Changing subject.)* Do we have any Sweet 'n Low?

JAY. Since when do you use that?

STUART. Today I want it.

JAY. *(Concerned.)* And you deserve it. But does that mean you gotta stop using the milk? I mean you can have 'em both! That's a pretty sweet deal—the way I see it.

STUART. *(Not sure if Jay is talking about them or the coffee, as he drinks.)* I'm lost. Are we talking about—

JAY. *(Metaphorically referring to his life and relationship with Stuart.)* Years ago, I loved my coffee black. Nothing in it. All by itself. Then one day, for no good reason, I added milk. Even though I thought— this is gonna dilute my caffeine high. It didn't. It added another "colorful" dimension. And I realized "coffee and milk—'it is good.'" Cuz coffee—all alone—can wire you up. But adding milk can be calming. So I wouldn't give up, Stuart—on the milk—in the coffee.

STUART. *(Lovingly.)* I won't. I promise ... Now, I am going to be so late for synagogue.

JAY. Then, go. See you tonight.

(Stuart kisses Jay, then races off as Jay stands there, concerned. Jay exits and lights shift to: A stressed-out Stuart racing on and talking to members of his synagogue.)

STUART. *(To audience.)* Sorry I'm late. I—uh—*(Thinking fast.)* overslept. *(Looking around.)* Aren't there ten already? *(Pleased.)* No? … Oh, so *I'm* the tenth man. *(Realizing what Jay meant—"something will happen")* No *wonder* you're all so glad to see me.

(Stuart takes out the prayer book and tefillin. Tefillin are two small leather boxes with leather straps attached to them. The hand-tefillin is placed on the upper arm and the strap wrapped around the arm, hand and fingers; while the head tefillin is placed above the forehead. As Stuart puts on the tefillin… An anxious Jay stands in another part of the stage.)

JAY. *(To himself, repeating Stuart's words.)* "What sinners we are. Just by being together, Jay." *(To audience, teaching at the Y.M.H.A.)* So, when you get anxious about something that you gotta deal with—most important thing—STOP THINKING SO MUCH! Just stay in the moment. In the present. Enjoying it. Not letting your fears get the best of you.

(Stuart wraps the tefillin around him and says the blessing for the wrapping. He begins to calm down—slowly being more in the moment. There's almost a sensual, loving quality to his wrapping, Perhaps the box on his arm touches his heart. It's reassuring.)

STUART.

Baruch ata Ado-shem Elokeynu melech ha-olam
Asher kid'shanu b'mitzvotav vitzivanu l'haniach—*t'filin.*

(Translation: "Blessed art Thou, Lord our G-d, Ruler of the universe, Thou has sanctified us by Thy commandments and ordained on us to put on tefillin.")

(While back with Jay.)

JAY. There's an easy exercise I give to my wacko patients—oh come on, lighten up. That's a joke, idiot!—to help them stay in the moment. At this seminar, we'll start by doing an abbreviated version. First feel your feet against the ground. Touching the earth. Grounded.

(Meanwhile a now grounded, in-the-moment, Stuart is praying the Ashrey.)

STUART. Ashrey yo-shvey veytecha, od y'hal'lucha sela. *(Translation: "Happy are they who dwell in Thy House, Forever shall they praise Thee.")*

(While Jay continues doing the exercise and explaining.)

JAY. I can see in your eyes you're doing it. Good. Now press your feet together. However you want. Just do it. Stop whining. Whatever's comfortable.

STUART. T'hila l'Da-vid. *(Translation: "A Song of Praise. Of David.")*

JAY. Heel against heel.

STUART. Aromimcha Elokay hamelech. *(Translation: "I extol thee my King, My G-d.")*

JAY. Soul against soul.

(Now Phyllis enters, with a mischievous smile and talks to her son as if he's out in the audience.)

PHYLLIS. *(Holding up fork.)* Fork.

STUART. Dor l'dor. *(Translation: "One generation to the another.")*

PHYLLIS. *(Holding up ball.)* Ball. *(She puts them behind her back in separate hands.)* Now where's the fork? ... No, no, that's the ball!

87

STUART. V'tsidkat'cha y'raneynu! (*Translation: "And they shall sing of Thy righteousness!"*)

PHYLLIS. BALL! (*Realizing she's screaming.*) But it's okay. Here, catch!

STUART. Poteyach et yadecha— (*Translation: "Thou openest Thy Hand."*)

(*Stuart takes the right strap, touches the strap on the bicep and then kisses it.*)

PHYLLIS. (*Phyllis throws the ball, suddenly thrilled.*) Oh my god. You caught it!

JAY. Feel your feet touching each other. *Enjoy* the sensation that 'hey, my feet are touching each other.' It's a nice feeling, isn't it? After all, your feet like each other. I mean, right?

PHYLLIS. (*To Ethan, can't believe it.*) Ethan, you caught it!

(*And as Phyllis just smiles out at Ethan.*)

STUART. (*Louder.*) M'ata v'ad olam. Halleluka. (*Translation: "Praise the Lord now and forever."*)

JAY. Let the energy flow between them. Till they're one. As if you've just got one big old foot.

STUART. (*With fervor.*) Halleluka! (*Translation: "Hallelujah!"*)

PHYLLIS. (*To Ethan.*) Well done! Well done! Let's try something else new. Throw it back to me.

STUART. L'dor vador halleluka. (*Translation: "from generation to generation, Hallelujah."*)

PHYLLIS. (*Ethan doesn't throw it. She gets upset.*) THROW IT!

JAY. (*Slipping out of the moment himself.*) Stop worrying if you don't get that feeling today. It's not easy to make two into one. Just—

(Stuart continues praying, lost in the beauty of the Sh'ma. He holds the four fringes from the four corners of his shirt together with his right hand and brings them up to cover his eyes.)

STUART. *(Sings.)* Sh'ma Yisra-eyl Adoshem Elokeynu. *(Translation: "Hear Oh Israel, The Lord is our G-d.")*

JAY. —let them keep touching.

PHYLLIS. *(To Ethan, calming down.)* I mean I'll wait. Whenever you're ready to throw it. Until then,

STUART. Adoshem echad. *(Translation: "The Lord is One.")*

PHYLLIS. I'll wait.

(And as Phyllis just calmly waits.)

JAY. Now guide this warm, tingling, positive energy up from your feet—to your calves—feel your calves.

PHYLLIS. (To Ethan.) You are so beautiful. And you don't even get embarrassed when I say it—because you know you are.

JAY. Let the energy keep moving up—to our knees—your thighs—

STUART. Al m'zu-zot beytecha *(Translation: "Upon the doorposts of thy house.")*

(Using the strap, Stuart touches the headbox of the tefillin and then kisses the strap.)

JAY. Slowly sweeping up to—your stomach. And to your elusive heart.

PHYLLIS. I don't know why others can't see how much fun you are. And beautiful.

JAY. Listen to your breathing. Just listen.

(*Long silence. Stuart is in the middle of the silent devotion, the Amidah, shuckling and periodically bowing while Phyllis looks out at Ethan. Finally.*)

PHYLLIS. (*Can't help herself, still pushes.*) … Throw me the ball, baby.

JAY. (*To audience.*) And if you're losing concentration, smell the air. Feel the air going inside of you. Going out. Keep breathing! Do whatever you can to stay in the moment.

PHYLLIS. (*Reminding herself.*) It's okay. I'll wait.

JAY. Cuz the more you stay in the moment, the less your head gets ahold of your fears.

STUART. (*Sung during the following dialogue below.*) V'ne-emar, v'haya Adoshem l'melech al kol ha'aretz. (*Translation: "And it has been foretold: the Lord shall be king over all the earth."*)

JAY. Nothing screws you up like thinking too much. Believe me, I know.

PHYLLIS. I'll wait.

STUART. Bayom ha-hu, bayom ha-hu y'h'ye Adoshem echad, ush'mo, ush'mo. (*Translation: "On that day, The Lord shall be one. And His name."*)

JAY. Now let the energy finally slip up to your head. All that positive, tingling, relaxing energy, filling your head.

STUART. Ush'mo ekhad. (*Translation: "And His name one."*)

JAY. Hold onto that … Good.

(*Jay knows what he must do. Lights fade on Jay and Stuart.*)

PHYLLIS. *(Finally, at this last line, beginning to mean it.)* I'll wait.

(Phyllis stands there—with more of a sense of calm—as she places a nice hat on her head and waits for quite a while as lights back up and we find ourselves in …

Synagogue Lobby. Another Saturday—weeks later. Chanting is heard in the background. Phyllis stands at the entrance, waiting. Searching. Suddenly she spots Stuart. He tries to look away.)

PHYLLIS. Good morning, Dr. Weinstein!

STUART. *(Not wanting to talk to her.)* Morning, Phyllis.

PHYLLIS. Two Aliyahs in two weeks. That's quite something for a relatively new member.

STUART. I'm honored to have them.

PHYLLIS. I hear you've been coming every morning to Services as well.

STUART. I'm trying to get closer to G-d.

PHYLLIS. G-d also believes it's important to get closer to your fellow man.

STUART. … Did you receive all the stuffed animals I sent over for Ethan?

PHYLLIS. *(Amused at the lameness of his question.)* Uh—Yes, but I feel you've been avoiding *me.*

STUART. Well, under the circumstances, can you blame me?

PHYLLIS. Yes. Because under the circumstances, I need some answers. I mean why did you barge into my house—pretend you needed a caterer?

STUART. It was completely inappropriate.

91

PHYLLIS. Still you did it. Why?

STUART. … I couldn't believe Jay was having another life without me. For some crazy reason, I needed to see what it looked like. I know it doesn't make sense …

PHYLLIS. No, it does … Why did you pretend to be my friend?

STUART. I didn't pretend.

PHYLLIS. Then why haven't you ever called me back?

STUART. *(From the heart.)* I'm ashamed of what I did.

PHYLLIS. … Oh. *(Stuart tries to walks past and heads to the men's side of the synagogue. She follows.)* So I'm being punished because *you're* ashamed! And why did you touch me on the cheek? Well?

(Stuart walks into the men's side. Phyllis starts to walk into it as well.)

STUART. This is the men's area.

(Knowing she's not supposed to be in it, she steps out. Although frustrated, she has no choice but to go to her seat. And as Stuart sits in the men's section and Phyllis in the women's, suddenly a beam of light crashes down representing the glass wall that divides an Orthodox synagogue in half—into the men's section and the women's section. Stuart sits down and begins to pray. Phyllis, on the women's side of the synagogue, does the same thing. Phyllis sits a few feet back from him so she can see him quite clearly. Suddenly a shaken Jay walks into the men's section.)

JAY. *(Muttering to himself, incredulous because of his standing.)* I'm an F.F.B.! A frum from birth.

STUART. *(Surprised, as Jay sits next to him.)* What are you doing? You never sit next to me.

JAY. Finally pleased with me? *(Again to himself, incredulous.)* I can't believe it. I'm a frum from birth!

STUART. Let's go outside. (*Jay doesn't move. Phyllis watches on the entire time.*) What's going on?

JAY. I was washing my hands in the men's room—when who stood next to me? The President of the Synagogue. So I couldn't help myself.

STUART. (*Concerned.*) Meaning?

JAY. I told him.

STUART. What?

JAY. —that I'm gay.

STUART. (*Wants him to keep his voice down.*) Voice.

JAY. You're the one who's never cared.

STUART. But now we're in a place of worship. Our synagogue. Where discretion—

JAY. (*On a tear.*) Yes, yes! Nothing too public. Nothing worse than public shame. Go to the prostitute in the next village. Phyllis wants you to be my whore in Kew Gardens!

STUART. ... Why did you tell the President? Who knows if Phyllis was actually going to say anything?

JAY. She had to eventually—whether she wanted to or not. To get back at me. Get a piece of herself back. She bleached the colors from my coat, but that wasn't enough. I'm a therapist. I know these things. Besides, why should I put her through doing it? For once—I told the truth. And you know why I also did it? Cuz I'm proud of being with you.

STUART. (*Touched.*) Thank you ... Although you picked a strange time to tell the President—

JAY. (*Grabbing Stuart's hand.*) It was exhilarating. My hands were shaking, but then I just stopped obsessing and let the words fly out! And the world didn't blow up. I'm holding you right now. No shaking. It feels nice—my hand against yours.

(Phyllis watches on.)

STUART. *(Sincere,)* Yes, it does.

(But then Stuart looks around at the congregation. Concerned that he'll be judged, he pulls his hand away from Jay's.)

JAY. That's all right. I'll give you time to catch up to my newfound freedom.

STUART. Catch up? When it comes to being gay, *you're* the baltshuvah.

JAY. *(Remembering, upset.)* My parents never walked the streets holding hands. My father never even put his hand around my mother's shoulder in public.

STUART. We don't display affection just so the world can see it.

JAY. Even at home in front of your children?

STUART. Well, that's your family's craziness—not Orthodoxy's.

JAY. But Orthodoxy encouraged it!

STUART. So what did the President say?

JAY. *(With disgust.)* The President. And I thought the synagogue was our extended family—only wiser.

STUART. Talk to me.

JAY. I also told him that I'd fallen in love. With a baltshuvah. Here in our own shul!

STUART. *(Concerned.)* Did you say which one?

94

JAY. Well, who else would it be? Not exactly a temple full of hottie-frummies!

STUART. *(Amused, though he wishes he weren't.)* ... Go on.

JAY. *(Taking his hand.)* Can I hold your hand while I say this?

STUART. I really wish you wouldn't.

(But Jay will not let go of Stuart's hand. Phyllis keeps watching.)

JAY. He told me—my Aliyah for this week—'perhaps someone else should do it instead.' I asked him if I would ever get an Aliyah again.

STUART. And?

JAY. He got quiet. I told him I've been with this synagogue for over 16 years. A respected member.

STUART. And he said?

JAY. Perhaps I should consider "finding another synagogue."

STUART. Oh shit ... Sorry.

JAY. Then *I* said they'd have to drag me out of here before I leave. *(Calling across the glass to Phyllis and glaring at her.)* Same as I'm not leaving Manhattan!

STUART. Jay, softer. And my hand. I really wish—

JAY. *(Doesn't let go of his hand.)* There are moments in every couple's lives—pivotal moments—where one of them needs the other to be there for him—where it's all about one of us 100%. This moment is 100% about me. Be there for me.

STUART. I *am* here, Jay. At least I'm trying. But in a relationship, it's never 100% just for one of us. The other person is always there. I mean if you were even a little aware of that—

JAY. What?

STUART. No, go on with your story.

JAY. After that kind of comment?

STUART. You're holding my hand. I told you it makes me uncomfortable. But you refuse to listen. You may want an old fashioned obedient orthodox wife but—

JAY. Since when? I mean I'm the one who gets you your coffee—and ties your ties! … I am going through an emotional breakdown and you're complaining that I need to hold your hand—

STUART. In our synagogue?! You don't remotely realize how self-absorbed you are. Not that I'm not, but yours is Olympic.

JAY. I'm in the middle of being kicked out of shul and this is the way—

STUART. (Firmly.) Let go of my hand. Now.

(Jay won't. Stuart pulls his hand away from Jay's. Stuart looks around and sees Phyllis watching on.)

JAY. I left my wife for you, Stuart.

STUART. No. Phyllis kicked you out. You had no place to stay. I should have insisted you get a hotel or find a sublet. It's my own fault.

JAY. (Dawning on him.) … Oh, of course … Now it all—You said you were a binger. Find one passion, explore it, then move to the next one. So you binged on me and now—off you go. You'll do the same thing with Judaism. You'll never find anything to anchor you.

STUART. Judaism has anchored me.

JAY. (Puzzled.) Was it just my leg taking up too much room? I can change that. (Stuart stands to leave, panicking.) If you leave now, this

96

will be the last time we'll communicate.

STUART. Where do you get this bizarrely haughty voice, making these absurd Old Testament statements? I wonder where that's really coming from.

JAY. *(Hurt.)* This is *me*, Stuart. Me!

STUART. *(Without rancor.)* You need to find your own home.

JAY. I thought you and this synagogue were my home.

(Stuart exits. Jay opens his prayer book and begins to pray. We hear the sound of the congregation in the background. Phyllis watches on. Although she hasn't heard all of the words, she understands the basic gist of what occurred. As Jay prays, he suddenly begins to cry. Then holds it in. Phyllis stands without even realizing it. He continues praying. For a while. Then begins to cry some more. Phyllis starts towards him, not caring if anyone sees her. She wants to comfort him, but is stopped by the glass partition. She stands at the edge of the light. Unable to go any further. But wanting to. As we hear the congregation's prayers grow louder, Phyllis continues watching on—seeing her husband truly crying. Wailing—while she's unable to get closer. Her frustration grows. Finally lights down on Jay while remaining solely on—Phyllis. Unsure of what to do. The praying continues.

Phyllis finally moves away from the glass wall to the front of the stage. She removes her hat. Then she takes off her jacket. She has a nice, but casual blouse on underneath. Then she removes her shoes. Stuart reenters in his own time—a later time—and space. He now wears a button down shirt, but no tie, khaki pants and either sneakers or cloth shoes. (His shoes must not have leather on them.) He carries in a blank piece of paper sitting on a plate. He burns the paper and places the ashes back onto the plate. As he does, Jay enters—also in his own world—similarly dressed—carrying in a plate with a hard-boiled egg that's been cut up into three pieces. He sits on the ground. Jay very lightly dips his third of the hard-boiled egg into the ashes. Stuart also sits on the ground and does the same. As does Phyllis. They eat the egg. Although they're near each other, they are all in different worlds. Alone. Lights fade on Phyllis and Jay. During this, Stuart stands and takes a small flashlight out of his pocket as lights crossfade up on…

The Synagogue, again. Evening. August. The synagogue is in almost total darkness. The chairs used previously in the play are replaced with benches or blocks—for on this night of Tisha B'av, instead of regular benches, men and women either sit on blocks of wood or on the floor. The cantor is heard singing "Lamentations" (Megillat Eycha). Because each congregant in the synagogue would have been given a small flashlight in order to read the prayer book, the place should be speckled with dots of lights. In this relative darkness, Stuart sits on a block, holding his prayer book. He reads and prays along, using his small flashlight. In this light, we can only somewhat make him out. Someone else quietly enters, sits on a block next to Stuart. Also begins to pray. Suddenly that person (Jay) puts his hand on Stuart's shoulder.)

STUART. *(Surprised.)* Ah!

JAY. *(Nervous, softly.)* It's just me. *(Silence.)* You haven't returned my phone calls or e-mails in weeks. Do you realize that? *(Off Stuart's look.)* I guess you do.

STUART. Why are you here? You know you're not supposed to come back.

JAY. The lights are turned off tonight—no one can see me. I miss you … Did you hear me?

STUART. You've going to get us both into trouble. *(Stuart moves to go.)*

JAY. Stuart, it's Tisha B'av. The saddest day of the Jewish calendar. The holiday where we're supposed to humble ourselves.

STUART. I know.

JAY. So let me humble myself…to you. *(Stuart returns to his seat.)* Oh Tisha B'av—as you know, baltshuvah—we mourn the destruction of the first and second temples. That's why we sit in darkness.

STUART. (*Accusing Jay.*) Interestingly, some of that destruction was the Jews' own fault.

JAY. (*Realizing Stuart's talking about him.*) You are absolutely right. Sometimes I am—(*Correcting himself.*) we are our own worst enemy.

STUART. Sometimes?

JAY. Okay, a lot of the time ... But as we commemorate the loss of the first two temples, we also hope that someday—(*Referring to Stuart.*)—we'll get the holy temple back in our lives. Do you think that's possible?

STUART. (*Torn.*) I wish it were. I just can't see it happening.

JAY. Because I haven't humbled myself enough! I need to lower myself further. (*Although it isn't easy for Jay—an extremely proud man—he nonetheless, moves from sitting on the block of wood to lowering himself further, now sitting on the floor. Stuart watches this in silence. Moved.*) Well, Stuart? I've lowered myself. For you.

STUART. Sit back up here—next to me.

(*Jay remains still seated on the floor.*)

JAY. Don't you miss me a little?

STUART. Sit back up.

JAY. We could find another synagogue. Maybe not Orthodox. Well?

STUART. You're badgering.

JAY. (*Explaining*) That's how Jews make love. (*Stuart laughs.*)

STUART. I miss you every day.

JAY. (*Surprised.*) Really?

PHYLLIS. *(In the dark, completely perplexed.)* I don't understand either one of you! *(Both Jay and Stuart are startled.)*

JAY. *(Stunned.)* Phyllis?! What are you doing here? This is the men's area.

PHYLLIS. And *not* the homosexuals. So what are *you* doing here?

STUART. I can't believe you snuck in here, Phyllis. That's so unlike you.

PHYLLIS. It's the only way I thought you'd talk to me.

STUART. I see … I've been a terrible friend. *(Overly seriously said.)* Just as Jay has done—I, too, must humble myself before you tonight.

PHYLLIS. *(Dryly.)* I'd rather you just help me out.

STUART. I need to start fresh. So, as much as I'd love it, I can't be your friend.

PHYLLIS. Oh please, I don't care if you're my friend anymore. Jay has been kicked out of our synagogue. We need to be his champions—go to the President—talk to him.

JAY. That is incredibly sweet of you. But I don't want you fighting my battles.

PHYLLIS. Whether I like them or not, they're mine, too. No one in my family is going to be excluded … Well, Stuart?

STUART. *(Torn, starting to go again.)* … The service is almost over. We shouldn't leave together. Let me go first.

PHYLLIS. *(Confrontational.)* Why was the first temple destroyed?!

STUART. The laws were being interpreted too rigidly for the people to follow.

PHYLLIS. That's right. There was no room for heart. For accepting people's fallibilities. No one's perfect in this group, but we're all trying, Stuart.

STUART. Are you telling me you're suddenly accepting of what Jay does?

JAY. You do it, too.

STUART. No, that was my past.

JAY. How did that happen?

STUART. You should know. *You're* the one who taught the concept of same sex attraction disorder.

JAY. Back in the stone age.

STUART. Even that Shabbos when you explained it—and I was mocking you—I thought, "he's describing *me*."

JAY. Don't lie to yourself, Stuart.

STUART. *(Changing subject, to Phyllis.)* … You can't really be accepting of Jay's lifestyle.

PHYLLIS. *(Torn.)* It's an unnatural urge. But … he feels it. At first I thought he should fight it. Be alone, celibate—

STUART. *(Jealous, doesn't want Jay with anyone else.)* That's what he *should* be! No more dating for you. We're not animals. We can control our actions.

JAY. But what—*you're* already dating women?

STUART. I am … About to … In the next few months. *(Reminding Phyllis.)* It only takes one.

JAY. Date women. Keep your true feelings locked inside. But one day, Stuart … Maybe not today … or next year … but one day …

boom. Boom! *(Tenderly tapping Stuart's beating and potentially breaking heart.)* Ba-Boom ... I know.

STUART. That is *your* story. My world is not so absolute. You can't accept that, can you? *You're* the one who's small-minded and limiting.

JAY. I never said you were small-minded. *(Beat.)* Did I?

(Seeing her ex-husband's pain over losing Stuart, Phyllis is filled with conflicting emotions.)

PHYLLIS. It's all so confusing. I look at Jay and think—of course he's a sinner. And if he can't fight his 'urges'—he should live a solitary life. On the other hand, more than anything the Torah doesn't want us to be alone. Life's hard enough. The Torah also says that you'll never be truly tested until you're with someone. Or experience the full joys of life—

JAY. *(Surprised by Phyllis.)* You *really* are amazing, Phyllis. You are gonna make *some* guy a terrific wife!

PHYLLIS. Sometimes, Jay you are so inappropriate!! It's as if you were raised on another planet. You just don't know when to ... to ... shut up! *(Jay is stunned into silence.)*

STUART. No, he doesn't.

PHYLLIS. Don' t *you* start picking on him. Not as if you've got a lot of moral wiggle room. Ruining my marriage!

STUART. You're right.

PHYLLIS. Ruining whatever friendship you and I had.

STUART. Very true.

PHYLLIS. And then the painful way you destroyed whatever was—well—between you and Jay.

STUART. What?

PHYLLIS. I saw Jay crying in the synagogue. And Jay doesn't cry.

STUART. He was crying?

PHYLLIS. I mean the last time I even remember him—When? ... When we found out about Ethan. So don't you start, Stuart.

JAY. That's right, Stuart. Don't you start!

STUART. This is how you humble yourself?

JAY. It's just that you've ruined everything that was good between you and me. Right, Phyllis? ... Tell him how special it was between me and Stuart. Tell him, Phyllis.

PHYLLIS. Jay, you just don't know when to ... You just don't know. Why is that?! Why? *(Beat. Phyllis changes subjects. In her own way, terribly accusatory.)* A few weeks ago, I was trying to figure out *once more* why Ethan became autistic. If anyone in my family— Then I saw another article about Asperger's. How it's like having just a drop of Autism in your system. The symptoms range—

JAY. We know the symptoms. I'm a therapist, Stuart's a doctor—

PHYLLIS. *(Not stopping, aimed at Jay.)* From not being able to look someone in the eye; having difficulty understanding proper body space—

JAY. You don't need to go through this.

PHYLLIS. *(Not stopping.)* Lacking basic social skills! Not dealing well with things changing—

JAY. Excuse me!

PHYLLIS. Talking overly professorial. *(That shuts Jay up.)* A general disconnect ... with people.

STUART. Phyllis, is this *really* what you want to do?

PHYLLIS. You acted inappropriately! So did he. Why can't I?!

JAY. It's okay. Say it. It's not like I haven't wondered myself why Ethan became autistic—

PHYLLIS. As I went through all the dysfunctional, anti-social symptoms of Aspergers, I realized—*(To Jay, accusing.)* You! *(Long pause. She realizes she can't do this to her husband. She points to Stuart)* … And *you* … And *I* … all have it. But we don't have the luxury of saying, "oh, I've got this disorder." Instead, we try and fight those weird things inside of us … I think G-d challenges *me* to—*(thinks it through)*—to have more compassion. And you?

JAY. … More self-awareness?

PHYLLIS. Stuart?

STUART. More courage. And willpower. Ten times more willpower. *(To Phyllis.)* I've missed our talks. How have you been? Well? *(Off Phyllis' glare.)* The Ukrainian woman, how's she behaving?

PHYLLIS. She must've gone deaf. She doesn't complain about Ethan anymore.

STUART. Maybe he just wore her down.

PHYLLIS. It might have helped that I filed a complaint with the city. You know it's illegal to harass a disabled child.

STUART. *(Surprised.)* That is the first time I've heard you use that word about Ethan.

PHYLLIS. Well he never *is* going to be normal.

JAY. And so damn what?

PHYLLIS. *(Looking at Jay.)* And *you'll* never be— Which is why tomorrow morning, the three of us need to go to the President of the synagogue.

JAY. Fine.

(During the following conversation, some of the flashlights go out around them.)

STUART. What is going on here? The two of you are suddenly braver. Or crazier— You guys are like Moses.

JAY. So you can be Aaron—in the background.

STUART. No. With you out in front, I'll be forced out there, too. And right now— When I became orthodox, my family thought I'd gone crazy. None of them talk to me anymore.

JAY. (Stunned.) Since when?

STUART. It was okay being gay, but being religious—! So this synagogue—

PHYLLIS. (Doesn't believe him, sarcastic.) Is all you have?

STUART. I'm tired of being different. Sure they know about my past, but if I keep it to myself—

PHYLLIS. Living a lie.

STUART. You can't be orthodox on an island! You need a butcher, a mikvah, ten men, and a synagogue. I'm trying to create a relationship with G-d. How do I tell G-d that some of his laws I'm going to completely ignore—especially now—when I'm truly starting to be religious. I have to start from a pure place.

PHYLLIS. I have an autistic son, my ex-husband is gay and his ex-lover goes to my synagogue. Starting from a pure place is not an option for me. I need every color I can round up. Mix them in ways that have never been mixed before.

JAY. (Slight bitterness.) Like my coat of many colors. (As Phyllis takes

105

that in:)

STUART. Orthodoxy could break apart because of us. I mean look at the Episcopalians.

JAY. At least they've got the balls to be dealing with all this. Instead of *us* — acting like some old world, shtetl Jews — bowing, scraping — not making any waves. Is that how we want to be — in our synagogue?! Don't think about the Episcopalians. Think about the Tunisians.

PHYLLIS. The Egyptians.

JAY. The New York State Legislature.

(Turning off his flashlight, Stuart stands to leave.)

STUART. They'll turn on the main lights soon. Both of you wait here until I'm gone.

PHYLLIS. Don't shut down your heart, Stuart. Not for Judaism. That's not what our religion is about.

STUART. *(Still torn.)* I know, but what other choice is there?! *(Starts to go, then disagrees that there are only two choices.)* I can't believe that G-d would force someone into an irreconcilable conflict without the *hope* of a way out! I just need to find it. *(Retreating into his mantra.)* Ha'yom — harat — olam. *(Translating.)* "Today — is the beginning — of the world." *(Exiting.)* Ha'yom harat olam.

(Stuart has exited. Jay and Phyllis sit there. Only their lights are on. Then in his frustration, Jay stands, whips his yarmulke off and throws it to the ground.)

JAY. Let's go.

PHYLLIS. No. Hold on.

(Phyllis goes for the yarmulke Jay threw on the ground. Then stops. She has another idea. Using the flashlight, she searches through a bin piled high with yarmulkes. Finding the one she wants, she holds it out to Jay.

It's brightly colored, the kind only children wear.)

JAY. *(Amused, insulted.)* What? You're handing me a rainbow yarmulke?!

PHYLLIS. Of course not! It's a coat of many colors yarmulke.

JAY. Oh, so you're *finally* apologizing for destroying my coat?

PHYLLIS. After all you've done, you have the nerve to ask *me* for an apology?! Why do I even bother? Why?!

JAY. Hold on. *(Jay puts on the colorful yarmulke.)* I'm sorry for what I've put you through.

PHYLLIS. Let's go. *(Phyllis starts to leave. Jay doesn't. He just sits there. Not sure what to do. Phyllis sees that he's not getting up.)* Come on. The lights will be up any second.

JAY. I know.

PHYLLIS. Tomorrow we'll go to the President. Take care of this. *(Still Jay doesn't leave.)* Hello?

JAY. I can't wait for tomorrow.

PHYLLIS. We'll go to his office, discuss all of this calmly and quietly —

JAY. And discreetly? Do it quietly — they'll never have to really deal with us. No.

PHYLLIS. What other option —

JAY. *(Dryly.)* To be Rosa Parks.

PHYLLIS. … Why do *you* always have to do these crazy things?!

JAY. It's what I feel. *(Phyllis starts to leave again. But she sees Jay sitting there, very much alone. She can't desert him. She goes and sits down next to him. He is stunned that she is doing this for him.)* I can do it alone.

PHYLLIS. *(Convincing herself.)* My family have been members of this synagogue for three generations. They wouldn't dare kick me out. Also, I'm a mother—with an autistic son. I'd certainly make a stink. This one time, I am sitting here. For you.

(They're both nervous.)

JAY. Hold my hand. *(Lost in her own thoughts, Phyllis doesn't hold his hand.)* Are you embarrassed holding it?

PHYLLIS. Hmmm? Of course not.

(And still she doesn't take his hand.)

JAY. Stuart was. He's definitely the Waspy-est Jew I've ever met.

PHYLLIS. *(Worried.)* You don't think that's why we *liked* him so much? ... Jay?

JAY. What?

PHYLLIS. I'm scared.

JAY. *(Warmly.)* Feel your feet. Against the ground. *(They both do it. It calms them somewhat.)* I think Ethan should be bar mitzvah'd here.

PHYLLIS. Bar mitzvah'd?!

JAY. I know he can't learn any of the material. So we'll be his surrogates. He can at least get up on the bimah. He deserves that experience.

PHYLLIS. The congregation will just gawk at him.

JAY. They do that already. This time let 'em gawk at him—as a man.

PHYLLIS. That *is* important. *(Really seeing her ex-husband.)* As a man

... The lights are coming up. *(Both are uneasy.)* Ready schmucko?

(They take each other's hands as the lights of the synagogue begin to come up. At the same time, the sound of many voices singing ancient Hebrew prayers slowly grows louder.

From the way Phyllis and Jay anxiously look around, the people are getting closer. And closer. Soon the music is deafening. They continue to sit there steadfastly anchored as they are bathed in a blinding, somewhat terrifying white light.

Then blackout.)

The End

Playwright Jon Marans

Photo by Adrian Sie

About The Author

Jon Marans' play *A Strange and Separate People* was produced by Daryl Roth and Stacy Shane at the Studio Theater/Theater Row, New York City and the Penguin Repertory Company in Stony Point, NY. Mr. Marans' play *The Temperamentals*, also produced by Daryl Roth and Stacy Shane, ran for over eight months Off-Broadway at the Barrow Group Theater and at New World Stages. *The Temperamentals* was nominated for both the Lucille Lortel and the Outer Critics Circle Award for Outstanding New Off-Broadway play and Mr. Marans was nominated for the John Gassner Award. It was a 2012 American Library Association Stonewall Honor Book in Literature. The entire cast won the Drama Desk Award for Best Ensemble and Michael Urie won the Lucille Lortel Award for Outstanding Lead Actor. Mr. Marans' play *Old Wicked Songs* was a Pulitzer Prize Finalist for Drama, included in *Otis Guernsey's Best Plays of 1996-97*, and won the New York Drama League Award (including play and both actors) and the L.A. Drama Logue Award. It was first presented by the Walnut Street Theatre, then in New York City by the Barrow Group, and then moving (produced by Daryl Roth and Jeffrey Ash) to the Promenade Theater where it ran for a season. In England, *Old Wicked Songs* started at the Bristol Old Vic, transferring to London's West End at the Gielgud Theater starring Bob Hoskins and James Callis. The play has been produced throughout the U.S. and has been translated and produced in over a dozen countries. Other produced shows include the one-act *A Girl Scout World* (Bloomington Playwrights Project), *Jumping for Joy* (Laguna Playhouse and the International Adelaide Theater Festival), *Legacy of the Dragonslayers* (book by Jon Marans, lyrics by Ronnie Gilbert, San Jose Rep), *Irrationals* (book & lyrics Jon Marans, music by Edward Thomas, Village Theater and ATA, New York City), *The Cost of the Erection* (Blank Theatre in LA) and *A Raw Space* (Bristol Riverside Theatre.) In television, Mr. Marans was a writer for *Cookin' in Brooklyn* and a writer/lyricist for the 1991 *New Carol Burnett Show*. In film, Jon Marans and Yuri Sivo were hired by Universal Pictures/Tribeca Productions to write a political/war screenplay based on Roy Rowan's acclaimed book *Chasing the Dragon* which takes place in 1947 China, in the middle of their civil war. Mr. Marans is a graduate of Duke University in mathematics and a minor in music.

Once Upon a Gay:
A Jewish Journey Through
the Ex-Gay Movement

Jayson Littman

Many people are surprised when I tell them I voluntarily entered reparative therapy at the age of twenty-one without pressure from family or religious leaders. I usually respond by telling them that during that time in my life, it wasn't a choice between coming out and conversion therapy; rather, it was a choice between conversion therapy and not wanting to live anymore.

After completing yeshiva high school and attending three years of black-hat-style yeshiva in Israel and Brooklyn, I returned to my parents' home knowing I had feelings for other men. So I did what any other religious Jewish boy in his early twenties might do: I called the local shadchan (matchmaker) to let her know I was finally ready to get married. After a year of interviewing young, unknowing women in their late teens in hotel lounges around Manhattan, I realized that perhaps I needed to work on getting rid of these attractions I had toward other men.

I sought the counsel of rabbis in Israel and Brooklyn (I would only trust the advice of bridge-and-tunnel rabbis, I told myself). As the first rabbi I had spoken to at the age of eighteen told me, my feelings toward men were "just a phase," but when he still insisted that when I called him back at the age of twenty, I decided to speak to further rabbis. An orthodox rabbi in Queens informed me that I just needed a sexual outlet for my feelings and that as soon as I'd found the "right" woman to marry, I'd be cured! Still not convinced, I spoke to another rabbi in Brooklyn, and after some deep thought, he mentioned that "everyone has skeletons in their closets, not just you." He further recommended that I not disclose anything to the girls I was dating, as I was forbidden to say *loshon hora* (defamation/ gossip) about myself. I tried telling him that it wasn't actual skeletons that were in my closet but *me* that was in the closet. I decided to ask one more rabbi, this one in Staten Island. After a long hour of going through all the possibilities of what one might do and what other rabbis have suggested, the rabbi flatly informed me: "I don't know."

"Well, Rabbi," I said, with my eyes lit up as if I finally had the answer I'd been looking for, "that's the best answer any rabbi has ever given me."

So, without finding the answer to a problem I thought needed to be solved, and with no satisfactory sage among the rabbis of New York City, I turned to the modern-day avenue for finding an answer to a halachic (Jewish law) issue that rabbis can't answer: Google.

Amongst the sea of Christian ex-gay ministries found on the Internet, there was one Jewish organization that helped men deal with their "unwanted same-sex attractions": JONAH, or Jews Offering New Alternatives to Homosexuality. JONAH was conveniently located across the river from me in Jersey City, New Jersey, and when I spoke to its director and was assured that I would be able to live the "normal and happy" life that I so truly wanted, I was immediately sold. That conversation in 2001 was followed by a five-year cocktail of weekend retreats, intense therapy, "bibliotherapy," journaling, and creating non-sexual friendships with other strugglers and ever-straights (or men who are forever-straight).

As JONAH was a new player in the world of ex-gay ministries and not yet large enough to create their own weekend retreats, we hopped on the bandwagon of available Christian retreats, with a slight dose of Jesus-washing. I'll never forget my roommate on a retreat called Journey into Manhood (even at that time, I thought that would make a great name for an off-Broadway musical), who was a Southern Baptist priest who was forced out of the church due to cheating on Jesus with another man. He insistently told me in his Southern drawl, "You know, Jayson, even if you do fully heal from homosexuality, you'll never fully be healed until you accept Jesus Christ as your Lord and Savior!"

As faith and G-d meant more to me than my sexual orientation, it was a liberating experience being in a community of men who felt the same way. It was exhilarating to leave the life of being obviously the "only religious person struggling with homosexuality" to knowing that others felt the same shame, guilt and fear of having attractions to other men. In some twisted way I felt that these experiences were my own "coming out," even though I was now beginning a process of repressing my feelings.

Over the course of those five years, I began to shed my "gay identity," as I truly believed it was a politically created idea invented by gay activists to promote their abominable lifestyle. One ex-gay leader at the Love, Sex & Intimacy retreat held in the Washington, D.C. area, a seminar to help heal homosexuals, would start his speech by saying, "Gay lifestyle?! More like deathstyle!" I worked through therapy to gain confidence, shed body-image issues, and work on correcting the classic triadic family dynamic (enmeshed mother, distant father, and confused, overly sensitive son) that resulted in my homosexual condition (so I believed). During therapy I learned how to love myself, love my parents, and feel emotions. I became confident, secure, and emotional.

I became close to other men around my age who were on the same journey, and often we would sit around and talk. I called the stage we were in "no-man's land"—there was an obvious literal meaning to that, as we weren't sexually active with men (or each other, to the dismay of most people who think that's what happens at these retreats), and we weren't attracted to women, so we mainly hung out with each other. We decided that we didn't appreciate the term "ex-gay," as how can we be ex-gay if we were never gay to begin with? We spent hours one afternoon debating what to call our in-between status, and when we broke down the word "ex-homo" to "ex-mo" and said it a bunch of times fast, we realized that it sounded like "Eskimo." We then segregated ourselves to Jewskimos (Jewish Eskimos) and Chriskimos (Christian Eskimos), which further broke down into Episkimos (Episcopalian Eskimos) and Methkimos (Methodist Eskimos). We never met any Muskimos (Muslim Eskimos) during our journey.

I was able to learn a lot from my Jewish and Christian brothers on this journey of "change." I realized that many Christians who were attempting to change had an end-goal of celibacy, while the Jews had goals of being married with children. This obvious religious difference had much to do with celibacy being highly regarded and practiced in Christian culture, while Jews focus on biblical procreation (also known as "pleasing our families"). Therapy was never focused on increasing our opposite-sex attractions, and this made sense: the founders and practitioners of conversion therapy were Christians, and a Christian who achieves celibacy in his therapy considers himself successful. This is not the case for Jews.

Another difference between Christians and Jews was our relationship with G-d. My Christian brothers idealized the concept of surrendering their feelings to Jesus, while Jews have always preferred the concept of struggling with G-d and free choice. Christians were motivated to change because they were told that if they were gay, they were no longer Christian. Jews were motivated to change because they were told that if they were gay, their mothers would not have grandchildren.

After going through five years of conversion therapy and completing all the tasks required to transition to heterosexuality, including, but not limited to, setting up profiles on Jewish dating sites and doing my share of pick-ups in the lobbies of Upper West Side buildings named after sunny places in Florida, I still felt, well, gay. I stopped dating women, usually responding to queries of set-ups with the common Jewish response, "Oh, I already know her."

The confidence I gained in conversion therapy actually allowed me to proudly come out as a gay man. The leaders at JONAH were quick to state that I was not willing to do "the hard work necessary to completely change" or that I wouldn't shed the "politically induced gay identity." Many of my friends in the Eskimo world deemed me a "dos-equis," a term I helped create for ex-ex-gays.

In hindsight I realized that what attracted me to the ex-gay movement was the acceptance of being a religious Jew with attractions to other men—a feeling I never felt those few times that I dabbled in the gay scene prior to entering reparative therapy. The ex-gay movement is a community of religious men who are affirmed by their religious orientation and find support from others in their continuance of being men of faith.

This made me realize that it is the responsibility of the LGBT community to embrace those who are still committed to religion or risk losing them to the religious ex-gay groups that will nourish their need for validation of their faith. While the religious and spiritual communities have hurt LGBT men and women throughout history, and the distaste for religion is warranted, our community must learn to welcome men of faith with more honor and acceptance; otherwise, we risk losing these individuals to the ex-gay communities that respect their value of faith over their sexual identity. If our community offered this same support, I truly believe that many would feel more comfortable stepping into the faith-affirming LGBT community. Our community can make the difference.

Advances in the acceptance of homosexuality in the orthodox Jewish world have come quite a long way over the last ten years—or perhaps religious girls have begun insisting that their rabbis stop encouraging gay men to marry them. It's not rare for me to receive a Friday-night Shabbos dinner invitation from a woman who wants me to employ my gaydar to determine the orientation of her boyfriend. Most Jewish guys tend to throw me off, as for years I've played the "is he gay, straight or just Jewish?" game in my own head. Of course, when the topic of gay Jews comes up at these dinners, I'm always thrown into a game of gay Jewish geography, followed by the hostess expressing a desire to set me up with "the other gay Jewish guy" she already knows, at which point my response is usually, "Oh, I already know him." You see, we really are not different after all.

Jayson Littman is the founder of He'bro. He'bro produces and promotes events for secular and cultural gay Jews in New York City. For more information, visit www.myhebro.com or contact Jayson at Jayson@ myhebro.com. This article was first published in *Heeb* and *The Huffington Post* and is reprinted with permission from the author. Copyright © Jayson Littman.

Wearing My Rainbow Yarmulka with Pride

Chaim Levin

Wearing a yarmulka had been a great challenge for me, mostly since I stopped identifying as an Orthodox Jew. While living in Crown Heights, I have walked the streets without a yarmulka, which many people saw as the ultimate sign of rebellion from me—the last straw and lamentable proof that Chaim Levin is not religious anymore. Many people could not understand why I refused to just wear it and show "respect" for the people in Crown Heights. My parents insist that I must wear a yarmulka while at their house, and I am happy to respect their wishes.

Wearing a yarmulka in public, on the other hand, has been something I have wrestled with for some time. I have always wrestled with the wind to keep my yarmulka from flying off. That inconvenience was not the struggle that drove me to stop wearing my yarmulka.

I could not understand why it was so important that I wore this thing to define my status as a Jew and, on the streets of Crown Heights, to be perceived as an respectful Jew. I often felt, if wearing a yarmulka were so important to the Jewish community, my parents and my grandparents who survived the camps and the evil reigns of the likes of Stalin and Lenin, I should wear a yellow star on my arm. While that might have been rebelliously, perhaps angrily bold and even offensive, it would have been something I understood.

The only rationale that I was never able to dismiss was that a yarmulka is a sign of identity; identity was something I was taught to proclaim and be proud of no matter what. Dressed as an Orthodox Jew, I walked around Paris while in yeshiva, despite the many issues I encountered from some anti-Semitic people.

However, I was kicked out of yeshiva after being identified as gay, and I encountered very many difficulties and alienation within the Orthodox community because of my identity. As a result, I wrestled with my identity as an Orthodox Jew, and eventually stopped wearing my yarmulka. Still, I was constantly reminded of it whenever I would feel the wind on my face and instinctively put my hand to my head in vain to protect a visceral part of me I no longer had.

I later learned, contrary to what I was taught, that wearing a yarmulka is not the exclusive signature of Orthodox Jews. Recently, I had the great honor and pleasure of meeting with someone who pioneered rainbow yarmulkas when we met to discuss my journey into the public eye and giving people hope. I was delighted and humbled when he gave me the yarmulka that he wore at his wedding this past July when he married his partner of five years. I put it on right then and there and felt like I never wanted to take it off ever again.

This rainbow yarmulka palliated the hole in my viscera and resolved some of the conflict I have been wrestling with. I have not wrestled alone. I am proud of the progress that gay people have made. I am proud of the gay Jewish people who have overcome their personal struggles. I am proud of, elated with and grateful for my wonderful parents and others from the Orthodox community I had believed would never accept me. Growing up Orthodox, I was taught identity was something to proclaim and be proud of no matter what. I understand that better now, and I am certainly prouder.

Wearing my yarmulka with pride, I have appeared in public for interviews during the past few months. I was surprised by some very harsh criticism and scrutiny that claimed I was misrepresenting myself as a fully observant Orthodox Jew. What I have realized is that wearing a yarmulka in public is a symbol of pride in my family, my Jewish heritage and the struggles Jewish people have overcome, and I am proud to wear my Jewish identity on my head. Others have suggested that the pride I have wrestled to find is an antagonistic ploy against the Orthodox community, in essence subverting Orthodox custom with the "gay agenda" right on the top of my head. If there were a "gay agenda," I would hope to be asked to participate, but it wouldn't change why I wear my yarmulka. However, there is no "gay agenda" other than in homophobic rhetoric, just as there has never been a "Jewish agenda" or Judenproblem other than in anti-Semitic propaganda. Still, even real agendas have little to do with the inherently personal decision to wear yarmulkas. My own choice to wear a rainbow yarmulka has nothing to do with how others might see it.

I wear my yarmulka because I am proud: I am Jewish and gay. I am equally proud of both identities and would not want see anyone discriminated against because of either. As time goes by, as more awareness grows and Jewish communities and the Orthodox community in particular acknowledges people who are different, people who are gay, people who are victims of abuse or authority—as light is shed on the precarious realities faced by people within Orthodox communities—I am more inclined than ever to wear a yarmulka and proclaim my pride as gay Jew. These two identities have been the targets of discrimination and violence for millenia and once seemed incompatible. My identity as a gay Jew grows stronger and prouder with each passing day. While I may not wear it all the time, I will always wear my yarmulka with pride.

Chaim Levin is a Jewish LGBT activist and blogger for *Gotta Give 'Em Hope* (http://gottagivemhope.blogspot.com/). This article was first published in *The Huffington Post* and is reprinted with permission from the author.

Permissions

Production photos of *A Strange and Separate People* by Kerwin McCarthy are reprinted by permission of the photographer. Production photos of *A Strange and Separate People* by Michael Portantiere/FollowSpotPhoto.com are reprinted by permission of the photographer. Photo of Magen David star glass painting by york777/Shutterstock.com. Photo of a man at temple by GWImages/Shutterstock.com. Photo of rainbow yarmulka by Konstantin/Shutterstock.com. Cover art and logo design by Adrian See and used by permission of the artist.

The English language stock and amateur stage performance rights in the United States, its territories, possessions and Canada for *A Strange and Separate People* are controlled exclusively by Dramatists Play Service, Inc., 440 Park Avenue South, New York, NY 10016. No professional or nonprofessional performance of the Play may be given without obtaining in advance the written permission of Dramatists Play Service, Inc., and paying the requisite fee.

Inquiries concerning all other rights should be addressed to International Creative Management, Inc., 730 Fifth Avenue, New York, NY 10019. Attn: Buddy Thomas.

SPECIAL NOTE
Anyone receiving permission to produce *A Strange and Separate People* is required to give credit to the Author as sole and exclusive Author of the Play on the title page of all programs distributed in connection with performances of the Play and in all instances in which the title of the Play appears for purposes of advertising, publicizing or otherwise exploiting the Play and/or a production thereof. The name of the Author must appear on a separate line, in which no other name appears, immediately beneath the title and in size of type equal to 50% of the size of the largest, most prominent letter used for the title of the Play. No person, firm or entity may receive credit larger or more prominent than that accorded the Author. The following acknowledgment[s] must appear on the title page in all programs distributed in connection with performances of the Play: Originally presented in its world premiere by Penguin Repertory Theatre (Joe Brancato, Artistic Director and Andrew M. Horn, Executive Director) in Stony Point, NY.

Lightning Source UK Ltd.
Milton Keynes UK
UKOW04f1359060315

247402UK00001B/43/P